Dior

NEW LOOKS

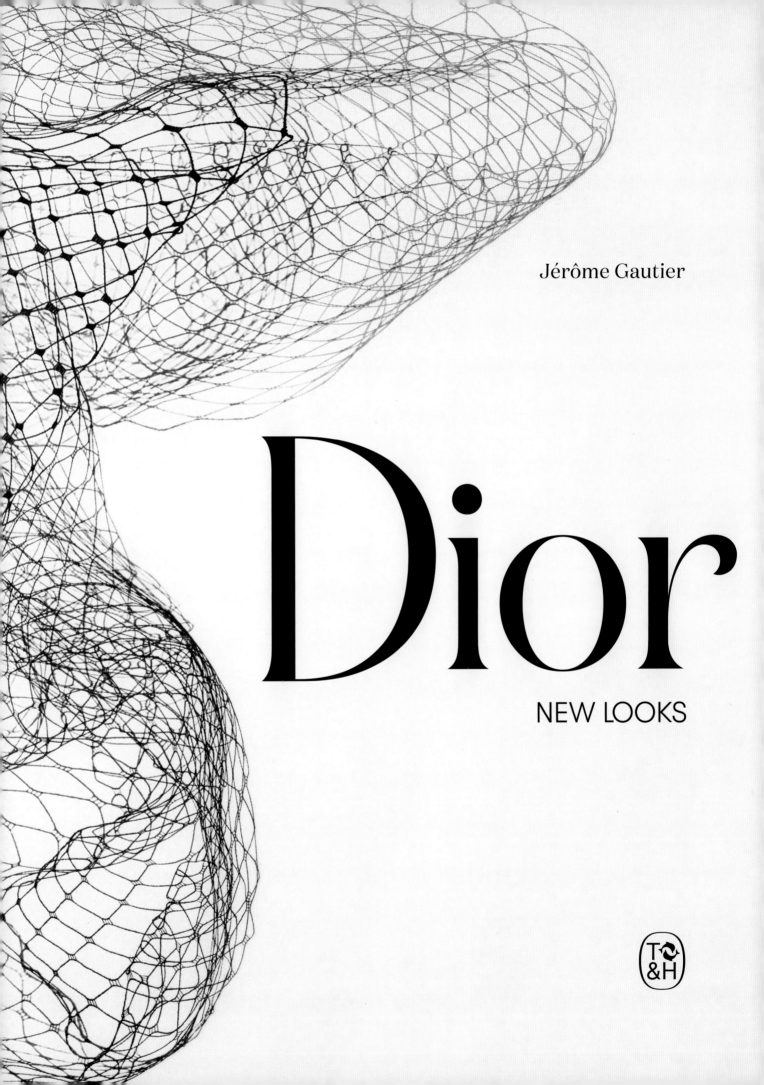

Jérôme Gautier

Dior

NEW LOOKS

T&H

Contents

Pages 2–3 **SØLVE SUNDSBØ** 2004

Left JENNIFER LAWRENCE **WILLY VANDERPERRE** 2013

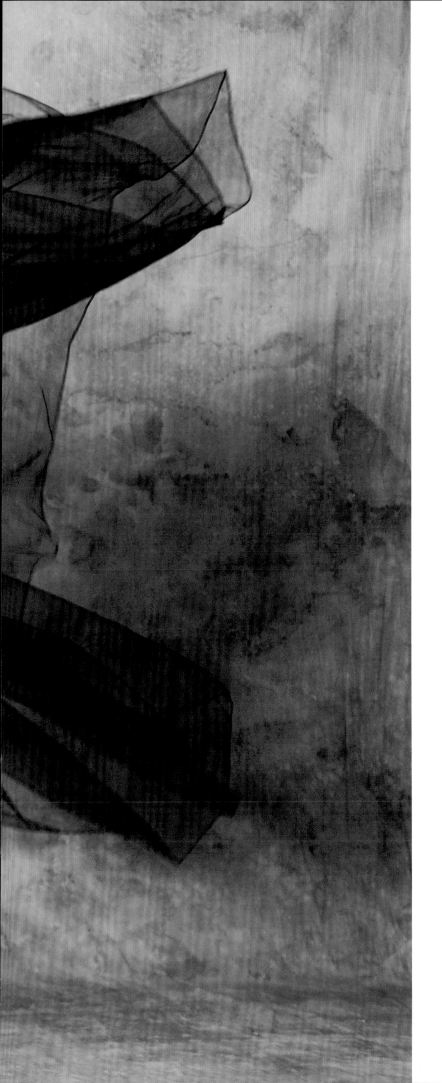

Prelude

The portrait of Christian Dior taken by Irving Penn in 1947 is an unusual one: it is hard to perceive in it the stature of the new high priest of fashion, the man whose first collection restored Parisian women's desire to dress beautifully in the joyful period following the Liberation and reshaped the fashion industry on both sides of the Atlantic. This was his first and last studio portrait, taken away from the familiar surroundings of his apartment on the Rue Royale or his couture house on the Avenue Montaigne. No models, no colleagues, no bodyguards: he is all alone. There is nothing to detract attention from this discreet, even secretive man, brought up with sacrosanct middle-class values that had been shaken by the sudden, brutal arrival of overwhelming success at the age of forty-two. Nevertheless, Dior had agreed to this proposal from Alexander Liberman just a few weeks earlier.

When he boarded the *Queen Elizabeth* at Cherbourg for a transatlantic crossing to New York, the first stop on his great American tour, Christian Dior met up with Iva S. V. Patcevitch, president of the Condé Nast group, publishers of *Vogue* magazine. Patcevitch was accompanied by Alexander Liberman and Bettina Wilson (later Bettina Ballard), respectively art director and fashion editor of the US edition; they had just finished shooting the Paris collections for their next three issues and were on their way home. 'I knew none of them very well when we set off, but by the time we reached New York we were firm friends…In such pleasant company, my habitual shyness melted.'[1] Dior therefore agreed without too much hesitation to Liberman's suggestion that he should be photographed by Penn.

Dior arrived in New York on 1 September 1947. He stayed there for only two days before leaving for Dallas, where at 9 pm that evening he joined Salvatore Ferragamo, Norman Hartnell and Irene Gibbons to be presented with the Neiman Marcus Award for Distinguished Service in the Field of Fashion, before a crowd of three thousand. He was the first French couturier to receive this honour – if Elsa Schiaparelli, who won it in 1940, is counted as Italian. He then went to Los Angeles, San Francisco and Chicago before returning to New York: he had an appointment on the nineteenth floor of the Graybar Building, the imposing Art Deco skyscraper at 420 Lexington Avenue where the Condé Nast studios were located, including those of Horst P. Horst, Richard Rutledge and Irving Penn. Penn, aged thirty, belonged to a new generation of photographers; he wore sneakers and no tie, but there was little else relaxed about him. His perfectionism gave him a fearsome reputation in the eyes of the cover girls – 'I remember one photo session . . . that was absolute torture,' Bettina Graziani later recalled. 'From eleven in the morning until four in the afternoon, I had to maintain the same pose and the same smile.'[2] *Vogue* editors such as Beatrice 'Babs' Simpson and Bettina Ballard found Penn equally challenging: 'I generally worked with him in his early days, my own enthusiastic approach to fashion sittings succumbing under his tense, anguished, soul-searching attack. The mental torture to which he put both the mannequin and himself left me drained at the end of the sitting.'[3]

Penn cast aside the stuffy codes of fashion photography to impose his own style: simple, direct, modern images. Penn did his own thing with no pretence, as attested in his portrait of Christian Dior. With no ornate sets or theatrical lighting, he placed his subjects against a grey backdrop and lit them with a bank of tungsten lights to imitate natural light. Between 1947 and 1948, the worn scrap of carpet provided by the photographer – this was shortly before he created his famous corner shots – was trod by Gene Tierney, Frederick Kiesler, Peter Ustinov, Elia Kazan, Bill Mauldin, Max Ernst and his wife Dorothea Tanning, Leonard Bernstein, Sir John Gielgud, Marc Chagall, Le Corbusier, Salvador Dalí, Louis Armstrong, Edith Piaf, Alfred Hitchcock, Christian Dior and many other intellectuals, artists and performers. In this stark setting, the poses were captured in meticulous detail and the subjects reveal expressions to the camera that are theirs alone. These photos hold an existential quality, at a time when Camus, Sartre and de Beauvoir were discussing fear, ennui, absurdity and alienation as determining elements of human existence.

Two faces of Dior are revealed by Penn's lens. One image shows him in long shot, not quite sitting and not quite reclining, deflecting the gaze of the camera and allowing himself an affable smile. In the other – the one reproduced here (p. 8) – he seems weary, serious, almost overwhelmed. One reflects the essence of his public persona, while the other creeps into his intimate self. Were these the two roles that Dior played in his own life? As he suggests in the title of his autobiography, *Christian Dior & moi*, published in 1956, a year before his death, there were two Christian Diors: 'He and I do not belong to the same world. There's no question of who takes precedence – thank God! – and I don't consider myself capable of taking on the role he plays. But we are different down to the slightest detail.'[4] 'He' was the king of couture, an international celebrity who could look into Penn's lens and savour his own success as his amazing trip around the US drew to a close. 'I' was a sensitive and vulnerable man, prey to doubts and anxiety, who had not forgotten the words spoken by his friend Christian Bérard a few months earlier, just after his first sensational show: 'My dear Christian, savour this moment of happiness well, for it is unique in your career. Never again will success come to you so easily: for tomorrow begins the anguish of living up to, and if possible, surpassing yourself.'[5] It is this second Dior, serious and thoughtful,

that we see in Penn's portrait. Christian Dior would never see it in the pages of *Vogue*, however, for it was not published until forty years later, in March 1987, to accompany an article on the anniversary of the New Look. It also featured in *Passage*, the retrospective of Penn's work published in 1991.

Living up to, and if possible, surpassing himself: such was the challenge faced by Dior as he set out to uphold his own interests, those of his house, his employees and his business. It is not easy to steer a steady course when your story starts with such phenomenal success: the New Look and its long full skirts swept away everything in their path. Nevertheless, Dior managed it. Between 1947 and his premature death in 1957, he dominated haute couture, the very top of the pyramid of fashion, providing objects of desire all year round for rich clients, professional buyers, the press and, by extension, dressmakers and women all over the world who waited for the latest news from Paris before cutting their patterns; prêt-à-porter had yet to be invented and Paris fashion was a matter of global interest. Back in September 1947, however, it was still far too early to imagine any of this. Neither Dior nor Penn could ever have suspected it. The American photographer knew the French couturier by name; he knew what he'd seen in the pages of *Vogue* and *Harper's Bazaar* and what Alexander Liberman and Bettina Ballard had told him. Penn photographed Dior before photographing any of Dior's work. He had not yet been sent to Paris to cover the collections. But Liberman was giving the idea serious thought.

In 1949, Penn indeed went to Paris to watch the haute couture collections. By August 1950, he had returned, to the Rue de Vaugirard, on the top floor of a former photography school with no elevator, in a studio with a glass roof. 'Always sensitive to possibilities, Alexander Liberman arranged for me in Paris the use of a daylight studio,' recalled Penn. 'The light was the light of Paris as I had imagined it, soft but defining.'[6] The photographer began to take a series of photographs that would count among the most memorable in his career and in fashion photography as a whole. With an old theatre curtain as a backdrop, Bettina, Diane, Régine, Tania, Sylvie and Lisa – Penn's favourite model, whom he married as soon as they returned to New York – posed in the best that Paris couture had to offer. US *Vogue* published 48 pictures in their five Fall issues (dated from 1 September to 1 November): an unprecedented move. Out of the fifteen collections that the magazine named as the highlights of the season, it was Dior that was most heavily represented with thirteen images in all, testament to the impact of his new *Oblique* line.

At the same time, not far from Rue de Vaugirard, Richard Avedon was photographing Dovima: Dovima at the top of the Eiffel Tower, Dovima in the Place Vendôme, Dovima in the little studio on the Rue Jean Goujon. Discovered in 1949 by an editor at *Vogue*, she had quickly risen to supermodel status – earning a record-breaking $60 an hour and the nickname of 'the Dollar a Minute Girl' – and had recently begun to work with Avedon.

DOVIMA, TUNIC BY DIOR, EIFFEL TOWER, PARIS,
AUGUST 1950. PHOTOGRAPH BY **RICHARD AVEDON**

Left **WILLY VANDERPERRE** 2012
Above **HORST P. HORST** 1978

So it was that Diana Vreeland and the photographer took her to Paris to cover the collections for *Harper's Bazaar*. The results, published in the September and October issues, were striking. Flawless and enigmatic – Dovima never smiled, in order to hide a broken front tooth – she wore the fashion of the day to perfection, and that meant Christian Dior: 'In one sense, Christian Dior made them all; during the postwar decade his New Look, with its wasp waist, sloped shoulders, and longer hemlines, reflected an exaggerated femininity that had vanished during the flapper era and the war years.'[7]

Richard Avedon had been coming to Paris since the summer of 1947 and the advent of the New Look. Working for *Harper's Bazaar*, every season he shot the looks that would appear in 'Carmel Snow's Paris Report'. Snow's love of Dior is well known: it was she who coined the name 'the New Look' after that first show in February 1947, a moniker that instantly went down in history. She always made sure that this new star couturier's designs were well represented in the pages of her magazine, particularly in images by Avedon. This young photographer, recently discovered by Alexey Brodovitch, captured Parisian couture like no other: in the streets of the French capital, its bars, restaurants and cabarets, by day and by night, surrounded by cyclists, playboys or animals, seized in real-life motion. The narrative nature of his images notwithstanding, the clothes, their lines, textures and details, always appeared enhanced, a fact that evidently pleased Carmel Snow.

The work of Martin Munkácsi – embodied by his image of the svelte and tanned Lucile Brokaw, running along the beach at Long Island in 1933 – exerted an unquestionable fascination on Avedon. 'He brought a taste for happiness and honesty, a love of women to what was, before him, a joyless, loveless, lying art,' observed the photographer, who likewise offered up a vision of fashion that bubbled with life.[8] 'I knew that in Richard Avedon we had a new, contemporary Munkácsi,' acknowledged Snow. 'I sensed that with his keen, seeking intelligence he would develop into far more than a striking photographer of junior fashions.'[9] *Harper's Bazaar* catapulted him into the fashion stratosphere and more specifically to Paris, much to Louise Dahl-Wolfe's chagrin. At the time, the Paris collections were virtually her sole preserve, along with Jean Moral, to a lesser extent; but Snow and Brodovitch wanted a new angle on the New Look. Dahl-Wolfe was fifty-one, Avedon twenty-four: the grande dame of photography could do little to compete with the freshness, spontaneity and unbridled enthusiasm of the young pretender.

As fashion changes, so does photography. Penn and Avedon heralded a new way of representing women. The golden age of couture inaugurated by Christian Dior also saw the emergence of new image-makers, while the dominance of fashion illustration came to an end. The star photographers included Clifford Coffin, Frances McLaughlin, Lillian Bassman, Henry Clarke and Norman Parkinson. 'Dior swept all this dowdiness away in one collection and femininity never looked back,' Parkinson noted.[10] The old guard nonetheless soldiered on: Horst P. Horst, Louise Dahl-Wolfe, Cecil Beaton and Erwin Blumenfeld also played a part in promoting the New Look in the most prestigious magazines. 'Every page has to have its own face, its own spirit, to catch millions of eyes or it's only a scrap of printed matter,' Blumenfeld stated.[11]

Between 1947 and 1957, Christian Dior continued to gamble his reputation by coming up with new lines for each collection that were striking and new, inventing the concept of seasonal themes and keeping the fashion world lusting for more. His sudden death at the age of fifty-two marked a turning point, not only in fashion but in its presentation. Haute couture would soon be forced to give way to prêt-à-porter, buzzing with new ideas to dress the women on the street. To stay in the game and keep couture alive in this ever-changing world, bold new designers would be needed who were in step with the times. Dior chose his successors before his death.

Yves Saint Laurent was clearly Christian Dior's spiritual son. When Michel de Brunhoff, the editor of French *Vogue*, saw the sketches that Saint Laurent had brought with him in the hope of finding a job in fashion, he thought the young man must be a fraud: the sketches were so much like Dior's! In 1955 Saint Laurent became Dior's first assistant and heir apparent, who took his rightful place as head of Dior three years later. Obliged to do compulsory military service, he reluctantly left before the 1960 Autumn–Winter collection, and was replaced by Marc Bohan. Dior had hired Bohan as art director of Christian Dior London not long before he died. Bohan brought Dior couture into the 1960s, introducing a youthful style that was reflected in his *Charme 62* line and the *Gamin* suit, a tweed two-piece worn with a beret adorned with lily-of-the-valley, Christian Dior's favourite flower, which would be photographed by Penn and Avedon.[12] By this time, Penn and Avedon had a host of new colleagues: William Klein, Bert Stern, Antony Armstrong-Jones, Jeanloup Sieff and the devilish Guy Bourdin and Helmut Newton. In the decades that followed, they were joined by Patrick Demarchelier, Paolo Roversi, Peter Lindbergh, Bruce Weber, Steven Meisel, Annie Leibovitz, Mario Testino, Mario Sorrenti, Craig McDean, David Sims, Sølve Sundsbø, Tim Walker, Mert & Marcus, Inez & Vinoodh, and most recently by Alasdair McLellan and Willy Vanderperre. Legendary names from the history of photography have captured more than fifty years of designs, proving that Dior remains timeless.

Christian Dior created the New Look and his heirs have continually reinvented it to fit the changing times. In another sense of the word, Yves Saint Laurent (1957–1960), Marc Bohan (1960–1989), Gianfranco Ferré (1989–1996), John Galliano (1996–2011), Raf Simons (2012–2015) and Maria Grazia Chiuri (since 2016) also cast a new look at Dior's legacy, portrayed in this book by fashion photography. The Christian Dior photographed by Penn in 1947 would today surely find cause for celebration to see how sharp his fashion, style and spirit have remained. The spirit of Dior.

Right **PATRICK DEMARCHELIER** 2013
Pages 22–23 **TIM WALKER** 2014

CHAPTER 1

Field of Dreams

The power of the New Look continues to inspire awe today. It transformed the contemporary idea of elegance and lives on because it calls upon what fashion deems most essential: beauty. A higher beauty was invoked by a man, Christian Dior, in 1947, an ideal beauty that has since been regenerated, season after season and year after year, by Yves Saint Laurent, Marc Bohan, Gianfranco Ferré, John Galliano, Raf Simons and Maria Grazia Chiuri. The founder's successors have tirelessly breathed new energy into timeless images, brilliantly weaving the fabric of Dior.

'The Dior archives are fascinating,' Raf Simons avowed in 2012. 'They are an endless source of inspiration. I have sought out the stylistic expressions and attitudes that still seem apt and modern to me today.'[1] Here the past writes the present; the collections bring back Christian Dior's memory, not as emphatic tributes but as evocations of a style and a fashion, of lines and creations valiantly launched in close succession from 1947 to 1957. Raf Simons celebrated the phoenix of 1950s fashion, adding a dash of originality and modernity to the history that the archives relate. To maintain the link he could count on the virtuoso skills of the ateliers. The guardians of the house traditions are capable of rising to every challenge: when Gianfranco Ferré joined Dior in 1989, he compared them to a 'Stradivarius'.[2] Although they are located under the eaves, as is often the case in couture houses, they form the unshakeable foundation of this haven of hand-sewn dreams.

Enter an atelier and you will discover the exhilaration of expert handiwork. Everyone is cutting, assembling, pinning, stitching, overstitching, sewing, tacking and shaping . . . The hours race by and the 'hive' buzzes with unflagging enthusiasm. Christian Dior demonstrated a 'sincere and tender affection' for the wizardry of these craftsmen and women 'who join their efforts with mine – whatever their part, big or small – in order to achieve the success of our enterprise.'[3] What indeed would the creator's talent be without the eyes and the hands of these artisans of perfection? What would the sketches become without these nimble fingers who know how to decipher an 'unbreakable code' of 'hieroglyphical figures'?[4] What would become of the idea without the matchless technique of the atelier's *premières* – first hands – the virtuosity of the *petites mains* – 'little hands' or seamstresses – and the admiration and respect of the apprentices? Where would the soul of couture lie without them?

Pages 24–25 **PATRICK DEMARCHELIER** 2008
Left **PATRICK DEMARCHELIER** 2007

To salute this spirit of excellence, US *Vogue* devoted fifteen pages of its October 2008 issue to the peerless savoir-faire of these ateliers that persists today. Photographed by Patrick Demarchelier, the feature opened with a shot of twelve representatives from the Dior *Flou* (dressmaking) and *Tailleur* (tailoring) ateliers. They are pictured in front of the House of Dior with a selection of dresses still at the 'toile' or white muslin stage, with Natalia Vodianova perched on a stepladder (pp. 24–25). Hand on hip, the supermodel adopts the New Look attitude of the cover girls of yore. Lisa Fonssagrives for example, the legendary muse who was married to Irving Penn, inspired this corolla-shaped design, the waist cinched and accentuated by a patent leather *Bar* belt. Here we are at the entrance to 30 Avenue Montaigne, the place where the whole story started.

On the morning of 12 February 1947, Paris was freezing. France had been in the grip of a cold snap for three weeks, with temperatures in the capital tumbling to minus 14 degrees Celsius in late January. The forecast announced a 'generally very cloudy and misty sky'.[5] France did indeed seem to be under the weather. The elation of the Liberation was now just a beautiful memory shot through with disillusion. At the dawn of a Fourth Republic that many considered to be very much like the Third, could there still be hope for a new society? The new regime lacked a clear mandate and was struggling to impose its vision. Reforms were slow-going and often disappointing. Reconstruction was sluggish, the economy was stuck in the red; the country was beset by inflation, housing problems, rationing and the lack of bread, petrol, coal and fabric. Hardship still seemed to rule, though apparently not for everyone. In the 8th arrondissement of Paris, a crowd of women and men stamped their feet as they waited impatiently on Avenue Montaigne that morning. Elegant despite the biting cold, they were not queuing in front of a grocery, but at the entrance to a grand mansion that stood at number 30, the Hôtel Millon d'Ailly de Verneuil. One could just see that they were holding not ration coupons, but precious invitations.

'Christian Dior requests the honour of Monsieur Lucien Lelong's presence at the presentation of his first collection at 10.30 am on Wednesday 12 February 1947, 30 Avenue Montaigne.' So read the card handed to Harrisson Elliott, chief of publicity, who stood at the entrance, by one of the elegant little crowd. The distinguished guest dressed in a tennis-stripe suit was one of the most prominent figures in the world of fashion. Born into the profession fifty-seven years earlier, Lucien Lelong took over his father's couture house after World War I, infusing it with glamour by dressing boyish young ladies in shirt-dresses whose hems barely skimmed the knees. He had also been the first couturier to turn a fashion show into a society event. A famous figure in Paris high society, his second wife was the beautiful Natalie Paley, daughter of Grand-Duke Paul Alexandrovich of Russia and first cousin of Tsar Nicolas II. As President of the Paris Couture Syndicate from 1937 to 1945, when the occupying forces wanted to make Berlin the centre of fashion, Lucien Lelong

Right **MARIO TESTINO** 1995
Pages 30–31 **WILLY VANDERPERRE** 2013

stood his ground: 'You can impose anything by force, but Parisian haute couture will not be transferred, neither in one piece nor in parts. It is Paris or nothing.'[6]

Lucien Lelong's presence on this special day in 1947 was only to be expected. Christian Dior spent his 'years of apprenticeship' with Lelong together with Pierre Balmain.[7] Hired as a designer in December 1941, the apprentice couturier had become Lelong's closest collaborator as well as a friend. Climbing the stairs that led to the couture salons, Lelong now discovered brand-new white woodwork, bronze wall lights with petite lampshades, and pearl-grey wall hangings – distant echoes of the 'Louis XVI revival' that prevailed forty years earlier in the bourgeois apartments of the Passy district, where the Dior family had just moved. This 'sober but by no means bleak simplicity, above all … classical and Parisian elegance' is exactly what the new master of the house had asked of Victor Grandpierre, the decorator for whom this was his first project.[8] 'Our tastes coincided wonderfully,' the couturier wrote, 'and we were both equally happy recapturing the magic years of our childhood'.[9] Perhaps Dior was remembering Baudelaire: 'Anywhere out of the world.'[10] Flee the rigours of the world and the humdrum reality of daily life to plunge into a world of *luxe, calme et volupté.*

On the first floor, Lelong and his daughter Nicole were greeted by Suzanne Luling, the salon director, who accompanied them to their seats in the front row of the *grand salon.* There, Lelong greeted the man who had succeeded him as President of the Couture Syndicate, Jean Gaumont-Levin. The oracles of the fashion press took their seats (*Women's Wear Daily,* US, British and French *Vogue, Harper's Bazaar, Elle, L'Officiel, Le Jardin des modes, L'Art et la Mode, Femme Chic*), as did the distinguished buyers of American department stores (Henri Bendel, Magnin, Marshall Field, Traina-Norell, Bergdorf Goodman, Neiman Marcus) accompanied by their designers, prestigious suppliers and the senior management of the Comptoir Industriel du Coton (CIC – whose founder Marcel Boussac, however, was absent). This VIP audience filled the two salons and spilled out onto the landing and the stairs.

10.30 am. The show was about to begin. The tiny *cabine,* where the models were dressed, was brimming with excitement. The six models, ready in their first outfit, waited for a sign from the boss, hidden behind the curtain that separated the salon from the 'backstage' area. *'Polo. Numéro un,* number one', announced Colette, a second saleswoman. Out came Marie-Thérèse, walking to the centre of the *grand salon* lit by the flamboyant crystal chandelier. Silence – there was no music at the presentations in those days. All eyes scrutinized the camel-hair coat and black jersey dress. A former typist turned Dior model, Marie-Thérèse blundered and came back panic-stricken, refusing to go back out – a backstage 'drama' that went unnoticed by the audience. Lucile followed, then Yolande, Noëlle, Tania and Paule; the Dior vamps twirled in *Cambridge, Voyage, Matin, Elle,*

Montmartre, *Petunia*, *William*, *Tir aux pigeons*, *Acacias*, *Club*, *Passe-partout*, and *Gag*. After the sport ensembles and the day suits came the dressy suits. Tania wore *Bar*, a delicate ecru jacket in natural shantung over a vast corolla-shaped skirt in simple black wool. Of all the outfits shown that day, this was *the* one: 'Christian Dior's Paris afternoon suit, *Bar*, holds the key to the new fashion.'[11] Reviewed, sketched, exhibited, photographed and displayed left, right and centre, today it has become a classic. But at the time, Tania did not know it. For now, she turned gently, swirling her skirt – how long it had been since anyone had seen anything like it! How beautiful she was, with her gloved hands and pretty hair pinned back under a plain black wide-brimmed hat. Created by milliner Maud Roser for Dior, it looked as though it had come straight from a Watteau painting; the coiffure instantly outmoded all the high Fontanges styles crowned with frilly fascinators.

'We were given a polished theatrical performance such as we had never seen in a couture house before,' recalled Bettina Ballard, the fashion editor of US *Vogue*, no stranger to couture shows: 'We were witness to a revolution in fashion and to a revolution in showing fashion as well.'[12] Another witness was Hélène Gordon-Lazareff, the powerful founder of *Elle* magazine: 'Over twenty years I attended countless presentations of collections, without ever feeling the atmosphere that reigned at Dior that day. Fashion was no longer a show but a unique moment of creation. We were passionate, mesmerized. There were many artists in the audience: Jean Cocteau, Marie-Louise Bousquet. I thought to myself: these people knew Diaghilev, and what we're living now at Dior must be similar to the experience they had when they discovered the Ballets Russes.'[13]

People expected something new, but not a revolution – especially since Christian Dior had declared shortly beforehand: 'don't expect too much from me. I am against all exaggerations . . . My dresses will be easy to wear. A dress is not made to be admired on a hanger or in a magazine, but to be worn with ease and pleasure.'[14] The couturier wanted to do away with the fashion that had prevailed during the Occupation, to cast aside the memories of the women he called 'femmes-soldats aux carrures de boxeurs' – soldier-women built like boxers; Dior imagined a new genre, 'flower-women'.[15] Indeed, *Corolle* was the name of one of the two lines in his Spring–Summer 1947 collection, in which the *Bar* outfit stood as the example, with a close-fitting jacket that magnified the slender waist, worn over an incredibly full skirt cut long and supple to create a delightful swirl of fabric. The second line was christened by Dior *En 8* (figure of eight). 'Clean and curved, the neck highlighted, the waist nipped, the hips accentuated' read the press kit: a radiant bust, rounded shoulders, a honed waist, a slender silhouette, heightened femininity. 'It was a generosity of plenty,' Diana Vreeland commented. 'The war is over, forget it.'[16]

SUZY PARKER AND MIKE NICHOLS, MODEL AND DIRECTOR, CHRISTIAN DIOR SALON, PARIS, JULY 29, 1962. PHOTOGRAPH BY **RICHARD AVEDON**

35

'Very soon, the entry of each model was accompanied by gusts of applause. I stuffed my ears, terrified of feeling confident too soon', Christian Dior recalled.[17] Carmel Snow raved behind her hat veil. The editor-in-chief of *Harper's Bazaar* had sensed there was a whirlwind coming with the Spring 1946 collections by Lucien Lelong, where streams of fabrics in bright colours put paid to the obvious desolation of war-weary haute couture. Seeing such free abandon from a house that had been averse to flashy flights of fancy had already convinced Miss Snow that the designer, whom she had met back in 1939 when he was working for Robert Piguet and from whom she had commissioned illustrations for her magazine, was remarkably talented. So when Dior decided to become a couturier in his own right, she rallied her troops. With a house in his own name, he would be able to give free rein to his fashion desires and boost haute couture, which was looking decidedly lifeless. Carmel Snow was jubilant by the time one of the last outfits emerged, a grand evening dress in white satin named *Harpers* – Dior had cheekily given some of his dresses the names of famous magazines (*Harper's Bazaar*, *Vogue*, *Femina*, *Figaro*, *Elle*).[18] Tania, who turned into a star model even before the show was over, twirled with *Bluette*, 'double *Corolle* line'.[19] Modelled by Lucile, *Fidélité*, the wedding dress that closed the show, was greeted with enthusiasm and thunderous 'bravos'.

A stunned Christian Dior was wrenched from the *cabine* by Raymonde Zehnacker, his trusted collaborator, Marguerite Carré, his 'Dame Couture' (an excellent technician who ran the three ateliers, two *Flou* and one *Tailleur*), and Mitzah Bricard, his muse in charge of hats – all of whom were visibly flabbergasted themselves. People rushed to greet, embrace and compliment them. Dressed in his conservative blue suit, Christian Dior received 'the compliments of the jury': Lucien Lelong, Bettina Ballard, Michel de Brunhoff, Lucien and Cosette Vogel, Hélène Gordon-Lazareff, Alice Chavanne, Marie-Louise Bousquet and, of course, Carmel Snow. Swooning over the collection, the 'head' of *Harper's Bazaar* proclaimed: 'It's quite a revolution, dear Christian. Your dresses have such a new look. They are wonderful, you know?'[20] Her protégé had conjured up dresses that were dreams in themselves and his vision was sharply in focus. Dior was elated: 'As long as I live, whatever triumphs I win, nothing will ever exceed my feelings at that supreme moment.'[21]

Since the salons were too small to fit everyone in, the presentation was repeated that afternoon at 3 o'clock in front of a high-society audience of 'women' ('in haute couture you don't say "clients", you say "women"', commented Suzanne Luling) plus celebrities and friends.[22] Two American photo-journalists were also present. They had clearly benefited from a special dispensation: at that time no photographs or sketches were allowed during haute couture presentations for fear the dresses would be copied. Pat English was the Paris correspondent for *Life* magazine, which had 21 million readers; Eugene Kammerman

Left **HENRY CLARKE** 1955
Above **LOUISE DAHL-WOLFE** 1953

was dispatched by the magazine *Collier's*. The two of them took a series of emblematic shots. English photographed Tania dressed in the *Bar* suit – a shot that shows something of the electricity the model generated in the audience: Carmen Saint, a young Brazilian beauty who had recently moved to Paris, and her two neighbours, stood up in the third row so as to not miss a moment; in the first row, Christian Bérard, seated next to other friends of Dior's, including Marie-Laure de Noailles and Etienne de Beaumont, could not take his eyes off the outfit; the wife of General Béthouart, Princess Sixte de Bourbon and Lady Diana Cooper, the wife of the British Ambassador to France who sat next to the film director René Clair, all looked utterly absorbed, while Doris Duke – the wealthy heiress of a tobacco tycoon – hid behind her sunglasses and exchanged remarks with Carmel Snow.[23] Duke lived in Paris, where she worked for *Harper's Bazaar*, and was therefore in attendance both as a VIP and a journalist, accompanied by her editor-in-chief. Carmel Snow had wanted to see the collection again, as though to highlight the very special nature of the event: the advent of Christian Dior, the genius and progenitor of a dazzling 'New Look'.

The New Look: an American expression encapsulated the latest Parisian fashion soon to be splashed all over the headlines. There was no way the clique of fashion-show regulars could keep quiet about what they had seen in this corner of paradise amid the prevailing doom and gloom. The world had to discover Dior: his name would explode like a star in the firmament of haute couture, his stunning ideas would bedazzle the clothing industry.

Ironically, the news first travelled abroad, for France was going through an insurrection of its own. General discontent was demonstrated by workers downing tools in many sectors. The year 1947 saw great strikes, notably in the press.[24] The National Union of Press Employees claimed their wages were lower than they would have been if the pre-war hierarchy had been respected, and they ceased working. The newspapers *L'Humanité*, *L'Aurore* and *Combat* stopped being printed on 14 February, followed the next day by *Le Monde*. The strike lasted a month, until 16 March. It was a difficult time for the new couture house, whose promotion in France was seriously affected. Dior's notoriety came first from the United States; fashion entered the age of media attention on a grand scale. No collection had ever received such coverage: does anyone remember the precise date that Paul Poiret flayed the corset, Chanel launched her little black dress, Schiaparelli her thick 'sportswear' jumpers or Madeleine Vionnet her bias-cut dresses, revolutionary though they all were? Wednesday 12 February 1947 is a date that stays tied to the New Look. 'There are moments when fashion changes fundamentally,' commented British *Vogue*, 'when it is more than a matter of differences in detail. The whole fashion attitude seems to change – the whole structure of the body. This is one of those moments.'[25]

By dressing women of his time, Dior became a couturier for posterity, and not just the history of fashion. The New Look inspired a collective passion on a planetary scale. It provoked rage as well, for above all, Dior came as a shock – more a moral shock than a visual one. The press wrote whole columns about the scandalous waste of fabric. The couturier's enchanting dresses jarred in America, where President Truman and George Marshall, the Secretary of State, were shoring up a recovery plan for Europe (the Marshall Plan was announced on 5 June 1947), which offered aid to parts of the continent to fight 'hunger, poverty, despair and chaos'.[26] The stunning luxury of the New Look guilelessly challenged a war-torn world worn out by misery. Christian Dior was regarded as a mean *provocateur*. Who would ever have thought it?

'Cheeky', 'unbelievable', 'arrogant' were the adjectives applied to the man who had caused the scandal. They were all wrong. Dior was by no means a troublemaker: in reality he was rather timid, kind and pleasant. He had an undefined mouth, a pointed nose, brown eyes, a balding oval forehead, a round face: he was a Mister Ordinary who assumed a sober style. 'I care very little about what I wear,' he confessed. 'For a man, the only real elegance is to not make himself noticed.'[27] In a suit that couldn't be more classic, which concealed a slight paunch, Dior was the epitome of the good old French bourgeois gentleman, a kind of Monsieur Perrichon, the character Eugène Labiche created in his play, *Le Voyage de Monsieur Perrichon* (1860). This was not something he tried to hide either: 'Monsieur Perrichon aux USA' is the title of chapter 4 of his autobiography, which tells of his trip to the United States in September 1947.[28] A few paragraphs later, he likens himself to the Fenouillards, hosiers from Saint-Rémy-sur-Deule, who went on a trip to Normandy and found themselves accidentally setting sail for America from Le Havre . . . The comic book by Christophe – one of the first to be published in France in the late nineteenth century – had fascinated Dior as a child, who still enjoyed chuckling over it.

He enjoyed making fun of his own image as well, which was quite at odds with his new-found fame – as seen on his arrival at his hotel in Chicago, where adamant demonstrators awaited him with cries of 'Down with the New Look! Burn Mr Dior! Dior go home!'[29] Dior walked past them in total anonymity: 'I do not know what sort of mental image they had formed of the hated Dior – they were probably on the look-out for a pin-up boy. At any rate, I passed through the hall without question, and my solid Norman looks aroused not the faintest breath of curiosity. All the same, I was a little disappointed!'[30]

Yet behind the 42-year-old couturier's good-natured air lurked a rebellious spirit. 'Temperamentally I am reactionary . . . We were just emerging from a poverty-stricken, parsimonious era, obsessed with ration books and clothes-coupons: it was only natural that my creations should take the form of a reaction against this dearth of imagination.'[31]

Left **HENRY CLARKE** 1956
Pages 50–51 **PETER LINDBERGH** 1988

The New Look would symbolize his uncompromising subversion against the fashion of the Occupation that was conceived in times of shortage. Parisian haute couture was in rags; he would strip it once and for all with the help of one man, the only person who could give him the means to achieve his ambition in such difficult times: Marcel Boussac.

From his father's cloth shop in Chateauroux, where he started work in 1905, to the creation six years later of the Comptoir Industriel du Coton, the cornerstone of his sprawling group, Boussac could pride himself on a giddy rise to success. He was the first to sell low-priced clothing fabrics in brighter and lighter colours than the dour bottom-of-the-range textiles of the time. It was the start of an amazing success story that survived two world wars and an unprecedented economic crisis. In 1945, the 'king of cotton' ruled over an empire of 15,000 people and was the world cotton industry leader. It was enough to underwrite the wildest ambitions – such as creating a couture house, for example.

From 1944, the Boussac group returned to a phase of unbridled expansion. The industrialist bought up or created partnerships with companies that no longer necessarily had anything to do with his textile activity, such as property firms. Meanwhile, he set about reviving Gaston, a fur and couture house he had purchased in 1928, which served as an observation post for Parisian fashion trends. Initially named 'Philippe et Gaston' (after its two founders, Philippe Hecht and Gaston Kauffmann), its salons on the Champs Elysées and later on Rue de la Paix had boasted a prestigious clientele, including the actress Huguette Duflos. The company went bankrupt in 1937. Now housed at 9 Rue Saint-Florentin, Gaston was no longer a couture house; it dealt only in furs and was more or less a sleeping beauty. Boussac asked its director, Henri Fayol, to find him some new creative muscle.

Much to Fayol's surprise, in late 1945 he bumped into an old childhood friend on the Rue Saint-Florentin, a chum he used to play with on the beach at Granville: Christian Dior. The two men had not seen each other for many years, but Fayol knew that Dior moved in fashion circles; he talked to him about Gaston, Boussac and the designer they were looking for. Dior thought it over but could not imagine who to suggest. He lived on Rue Royale, close to Rue Saint-Florentin, where he bumped into Fayol again, still on a quest for a one-in-a-million designer. They missed their chance a second time. The third time, however, turned out to be lucky.

Dior had been mulling over his ambitions and future ever since Pierre Balmain, his colleague and fellow designer, had left Lucien Lelong to set up his own couture house and present his first collection under his own name in October 1945. 'Pierre Balmain was the excitement of the Paris couture showings. "Enchanting" and "pretty" were the adjectives most often heard during the showing.'[32] So when Dior bumped into Fayol for the third time, he ventured a proposal without realizing he was writing his own destiny: 'After all this, would I do?'[33]

FRANZ CHRISTIAN GUNDLACH 1962

The first visit was a let-down, however. 'As I left Gaston, I decided that I was not meant by nature to raise corpses from the dead.'[34] Dior was determined to stay with Lelong. Yet the following day he set out on quite a different tack when he met with Boussac : he did not want Gaston but would be fully willing to create a house in his own name. There was nothing spontaneous about his proposal: the level-headed Dior had thought through his ambitious project very carefully. 'After the long war years of stagnation, I believed that there was a genuine unsatisfied desire abroad for something new in fashion. In order to meet this demand, French couture would have to return to the traditions of great luxury: which was why I envisaged my house as a craftsman's workshop, rather than a clothes factory.'[35] After considering the question, the textile industry magnate agreed to take up the couturier's bold but feasible bet: Boussac's group provided the capital to the tune of 5 million francs – an incredible amount at the time, but a New Look naturally would require ample means.[36] 'The thing about Dior that convinced me outright,' noted Boussac, 'is that he had a very specific idea about what he wanted to create and took great care over every detail. And beauty allows for no errors.'[37]

The Maison Christian Dior was created on 8 October 1946. Dior had tendered his resignation in July 1946 and left Lelong on 1 December to design his future collection at the house of his friends Pierre and Carmen Colle, who lived in Fleury-en-Bière in Fontainebleau forest. Among his early collaborators were Carmen Colle – who would run the Colifichets boutique and network her extensive circle of friends; Suzanne Luling and Nicole Rousseau, two childhood friends who were promoted to salon director and saleswoman respectively, Raymonde Zehnacker, a friend from his Lelong days, Mitzah Bricard, another friend who worked with Molyneux before the war; Marguerite Carré, Jean Patou's marvellous milliner, plus a handful of experienced workers, headed by Monique, Christiane and Pierre Cardin – a very gifted 24-year-old tailor; and lastly six models, including Tania, who also came from Lelong. The adventure got off to a flying start 'under conditions of unbelievable difficulty', with the *générale*, i.e., the first presentation, set for 12 February.[38]

A few days ahead of the show, fear, anxiety and doubt wracked the salons, which resembled a central design laboratory: the six models tried on outfit after outfit in the early stages of confection: 'thousands of different fittings imposed such a nervous and physical strain'.[39] Dior hesitated. 'He didn't know if he wanted skirts long or short – the postwar fashion was relatively short,' Pierre Cardin recalls. 'So we made everything short, then he says: "*Ah non, mon petit Pierre*, we'll need them much longer." We had cut the dresses at knee length, so fabric had to be re-ordered. But it was very difficult to get an extra metre of fabric at the time.'[40] This glut of fine fabrics would turn out to be an antidote to the blues in the economy – and so what if it upset some people? The couturier had the means to fulfil his ambitions and he had Boussac's blessing as well.

Rumours started to fly around Paris, boding well for the show's success. The couture house's public relations had done their job. Suzanne Luling had spoken to Jeanne Perkins, the correspondent of the highly respected *Women's Wear Daily*, who announced the opening of the couture house in its columns, with a portrait of the couturier to boot.[41] Christian Dior's friends were well connected in intellectual and society circles and added to the buzz. Christian Bérard, Etienne de Beaumont, Mrs Jean Larivière, Marie-Louise Bousquet (*Harper's Bazaar*), Michel de Brunhoff (French *Vogue*), Hélène Gordon-Lazareff (*Elle*) and James de Coquet (*Le Figaro*) let slip a few secrets about the collection: 'You will see,' said Bérard to Bettina Ballard from US *Vogue* while sketching some of the models on a tablecloth in a restaurant, 'Christian Dior is going to change the whole fashion look when he opens tomorrow. He's making huge pleated skirts like those the Marseilles fishwives wear, long, like this, and with tiny bodices and tiny hats.'[42] All this meant people's curiosity rose in a crescendo.

Christian Dior became a celebrity overnight – the first 'popular' couturier.[43] Not that he was unanimously hailed, however: 'Piguet was livid because we had to redo a half-season with the new length,' recalled Marc Bohan, who was working for the rival house where Dior started out in 1939.[44] The new couturier flew in the face of his critics and stayed set on his vision, presenting 'sapling-women' and 'flower-women' again in August 1947. The line of the second collection was even named *Corolle* again (the only time he used the name of a line twice) and this time the dresses hung just 30 cm (12 inches) from the floor, 'the new length revealing all the mystery of the leg.'[45] Like all the guests present at the *générale*, stars such as Marlene Dietrich, Dany Robin and Michèle Alfa felt obliged to renew their wardrobe – Marlene ordered ten dresses! Men, too, were full of admiration. Some people raved or raged as they left, others proclaimed Dior's genius. The Americans had reservations, of course, then got in line. The *Margrave* dress became 'the most popular dress in America'.[46] It was not long before everyone had to adopt the silhouette launched by Christian Dior: Pierre Balmain, Jacques Fath, Marcel Rochas, Jean Dessès and even the American couturier Charles James, who was fighting the ready-made garment invasion back home and travelled to Paris in July 1947 to present twenty dresses to French couturiers.

The New Look was now in vogue and the phrase became a label. *Elle* magazine wrote of 'Super-new-look' sunglasses, or that 'the Opera has the New Look', or 'the lady Minister has the New Look' in reference to Germaine Poinso-Chapuis, the Minister for Public Health.[47] The department store buyers who were selling Dior models around the world kowtowed to the team at Avenue Montaigne, smiling profusely with their chequebooks at the ready. Dior dresses racked up millions of dollars for France all by themselves. *Drags*, a navy-blue woollen dress from the Spring–Summer 1948 collection, was sold over seventy times (a record), which meant that France could buy 9,800 sacks of wheat from the United States.[48]

Left **PATRICK DEMARCHELIER** 1998
Pages 62–63 **PATRICK DEMARCHELIER** 2011

Haute couture ranked third in the French export industries (after wine and perfumes) and in 1949 the House of Dior single-handedly represented 75 per cent of haute couture exports.[49] The couturier had won the war; he reigned supreme while his name turned into a 'global' superbrand. Dior was more than a surname, it was synonymous with elegance and taste *à la française*.

As the great satirical playwright Molière once had a character remark, 'It would be the very antipodes of reason not to confess that Paris is the grand cabinet of marvels' (*Les Précieuses ridicules*, 1659).[50] Now the City of Light came back to life and turned into an open-air photography studio, the Paris of quaysides and empty cobbled streets, of museums and bistros, of jewelers and couturiers. The Paris by day and by night that goes so beautifully with the woman who embodies its spirit to the letter: *la Parisienne*. Fashion photographers followed her every step, from the Concorde to the Marais, Montmartre to the Tuileries, Montaigne to Vendôme. The references were smart and popular all mixed together, in the image of a Parisian woman who is elegant and cocky rolled into one. Dovima, Suzy Parker, Anne Saint-Marie, Mary Jane Russell – Americans born and bred – or Bettina, freshly arrived from Brittany, all represented the *jolie môme*, the pretty little kid from Paris, glamorous and casual, the expression of light-hearted spirit and chic. Without corresponding to any formal stereotype, she undoubtedly has style and even a certain *je ne sais quoi*. She has allure, she is couture and, above all, she rules fashion.

The collections were made in tribute to this Parisian woman who dressed in the latest fashion. In February 1949, Christian Dior paid tribute to the capital. His outfits were named *Métro*, *Bistro*, *Maxim's* or *Avenue Montaigne*, the avenue where all Parisians – native or adopted – now had a new kingdom: the House of Dior, a 'repository of the marvellous' in which the glass, the mirrors, the crystal chandeliers, the legendary images of the great photographers and the eyes of the couturier himself, all reflect and celebrate Parisian beauty.[51]

Right **ALASDAIR MCLELLAN** 2012
Pages 66–67 **WILLY VANDERPERRE** 2013

CHAPTER 2

Strike a Pose!

In the April 1954 issue of *Harper's Bazaar*, an image caught Christian Dior's eye. It was the portrait of Marella Agnelli by Richard Avedon. She struck a regal pose, standing in profile but with her face turned to the camera and her eyes smouldering. Dior was impressed by this mysterious, slender beauty. He had started to think about his next collection, now here was the inspiration. This photograph gave him the idea for what would be his next line, the *H* line – the most commented upon and criticized line since *Corolle* and *En 8* had introduced the New Look in 1947. As Carmel Snow recounted: 'With dash and style he had created a slim, elegant, ethereal woman. She suggests the beauties of the Italian Renaissance with their supple, slanting stance – and Dior, when I congratulated him, told me his inspiration had come from the Avedon photograph of Signora Gianni Agnelli, with her long, slender Cinquecento looks, published in the April issue of *Harper's Bazaar*.'[1] While the photographer may have inspired one of the couturier's most emblematic lines, one year later it was a Dior dress that featured at the centre of one of Avedon's most famous shots: *Dovima with Elephants*.

Dovima with Elephants. A photograph with a title says something about its value. The gelatin silver print mounted on linen, signed and printed in 1978 in a unique format (216.8 x 166.7 cm), was auctioned by Christie's on 20 November 2010 for €841,000. Following the photographer's death in 2004, *Dovima with Elephants* left Richard Avedon's lair for good. For twenty-five years it occupied pride of place in the entrance to his Upper East Side studio: he never wanted to let the shot out of his sight. It was a vibrant memory of Dovima and an eloquent reminder of his *Harper's Bazaar* years, the magnificent vestiges of a triumphant haute couture.

In midsummer 1955, Richard Avedon and Dovima roamed the streets of Paris to report on the collections for the next issues of *Harper's Bazaar*. The September issue was set to show the influence wielded over the collections by the two unchallenged masters of couture: Dior and Balenciaga.[2] The photographer and his model walked from the Grand Palais to the Place de la Concorde and the terraces of the Deux Magots, Fouquet's, Chez Yvonne and Maxim's – the seminally Parisian sites that the American readers of the elegant review had grown accustomed to seeing in its pages. This time, however, Avedon wanted to bring something else back from his trip, something surprising and unexpected, the likes of which had never been seen. In the early afternoon of 30 July, the photographer took his

DOVIMA WITH ELEPHANTS, EVENING DRESS BY DIOR, CIRQUE D'HIVER, PARIS, AUGUST 1955. PHOTOGRAPH BY **RICHARD AVEDON** model to the Cirque d'Hiver (the winter circus), which was the talk of Hollywood since Carol Reed was using it as his location to shoot *Trapeze*, starring Burt Lancaster, Tony Curtis and Gina Lollobrigida. Avedon portrayed nothing of the superproduction, however; he was far more interested in the incredible animals that Joseph, one of the Bouglione brothers who owned the site, had showed him in the menagerie: 'I saw the elephants under an enormous skylight and in a second I knew.'[3]

Avedon knew that he had found the unique location he had been looking for, the 'likes of which had never been seen'. He knew of the photographs by Munkácsi and Louise Dahl-Wolfe that had been published in *Harper's Bazaar*, of course, depicting models who looked rather like elephants.[4] But Avedon wanted something else – to see his model in among the elephants, dressed in an haute couture gown. 'I then had to find the right dress', he remembered, 'and I knew there was a potential here for a kind of dream image,'[5] something that would create another surprise for his mentor, Brodovich, who always used to say: 'If you look through your camera and see an image you've seen before, don't click the shutter.'[6]

Dovima rose to Avedon's new challenge without flinching. 'He asked me to do the most unlikely things and I did them because I knew I would be in a fabulous photo.'[7] There she stands in a Dior evening gown, a figure-hugging sheath dress, surrounded by Frida, Marie, Jenny, Tarzan and Jumbo the elephants.[8] When Sampion Bouglione, one of Joseph's sons, gave the command, the elephants lifted a foot and raised their trunks, the cover girl accompanied them with a perfectly matched flourish of her long gloved arms, all captured by Avedon's lens. 'Dovima understood what I wanted and did it so beautifully,' he recalled years later.[9] His preferred model felt the same way: 'we had become real Siamese twins and I knew what he wanted before he even opened his mouth.'[10]

Dovima next donned a black velvet sheath dress with close-fitting arms, a plunging neckline and a white satin band tied in a bow at the waist.[11] She struck pose after pose until she hit upon the perfect mix between the rough hides of the elephants and the sinuous fragility of her own silhouette. The contrast was striking and Avedon was thrilled: 'Don't move!' He had his shot. It portrays Dovima craning her long, swanlike neck, her right hand gently placed on Frida's trunk and her left hand held out to Marie in a triumphant Y – Y was the name Christian Dior had given the line he designed for Winter 1955. The celebrated photographer nonetheless harboured one regret: 'I don't know why I didn't have the sash blowing out to the left to complete the line of the picture. The picture will always be a failure to me because that sash is not out there.'[12]

The two shots were published in the September 1955 issue of *Harper's Bazaar*, pages 214 and 215. Suffice to say that they surprised and shocked what was still a highly codified and consensual world of haute couture – who would have thought of presenting evening gowns in a hay-strewn menagerie? The future, however, proved Avedon's boldness right.

Above **NICK KNIGHT** 1994
Right **GUY BOURDIN** 1966

Left **DAVID SIMS** 2002
Above **NORMAN PARKINSON** 1975

Dovima with Elephants would travel far beyond the pages of the magazine and become legendary. In the photographer's first book, *Observations*, published four years later, the texts by Truman Capote introduced some of the twentieth century's most famous figures, citing a certain Patrick Conway: 'A beautiful woman, beautifully elegant, impresses us as art does, changes the weather of our spirit: and that, is that a frivolous matter? I think not.'[13] While this point of view applies to many of the fashion pictures and portraits of women that the photographer shot during his prolific career, it certainly fits *Dovima with Elephants* like a glove.

Dorothy Juba, alias Dovima, the daughter of a police officer from the poor New York district of Queens, represented the quintessential elegance of the 1950s.[14] She possessed the idealized aristocratic beauty that could suitably magnify Parisian haute couture. In *Dovima with Elephants* she took on a typical pose adopted by models at the time and borrowed from classical dance: the fifth position, where the heel of the front foot touches the toe of the back foot. With her right leg poised in front of her left leg, Dovima accentuated the narrow fit of the dress while her velvet-clad figure portrayed the slim, sinuous line that was a hallmark of Dior designs. 'She had the most extraordinary sense of ease,' Avedon noted. 'She didn't have an overpowering energy but neither was she timid. And she had an understanding, a feeling for the clothes.'[15]

Dovima and her peers adopted this ultra-sophisticated pose in all the pages of 'couture' magazines, the most sumptuous of which naturally included *Harper's Bazaar* and *Vogue*. The latter unwittingly gave its name decades later to 'voguing', a dance that arose in the 1960s in Harlem's drag ball culture. Drag queens on the podium would perform exaggerated parodies of the great models' elegant poses. Popularized by the dancer Willi Ninja, in the late 1980s 'voguing' made its way out of the underground ball scene and into New York's hip clubs (Tunnel, Elk's Lodge, Track and World in New York, Daisy Chain in London). In 1990, Madonna even turned it into a hit song: *Vogue*.

The shots of the New Look glamour goddesses inspired the photography messiahs of the 1990s to turn top models into cover girls. Steven Meisel, who had been obsessed since the tender age of ten with fashion and its beautifully turned-out poster girls, asked his models to interpret Dovima, Lisa Fonssagrives, Dorian Leigh, Suzy Parker and Jean Patchett. Blonde, brunette or redhead, his favourite model Linda Evangelista went to town: the zeitgeist of the supermodel era perfectly captured the old-fashioned beauty that lived in the fantasies of Meisel, who was the first to openly reinterpret the images of Horst P. Horst, Irving Penn and Richard Avedon. The same references would crop up in the work of other photographers, such as Patrick Demarchelier, Peter Lindbergh and Mario Testino.

Avedon and Penn's works amazed, fascinated and inspired contemporary designers as well, notably John Galliano, who made a name for himself in Paris, where he presented

his first collection in 1990. 'I wanted to go back to the atmosphere of the early 1950s, the atmosphere of Irving Penn's photos,'[16] he declared after presenting seventeen outfits in a 'couture' show held in a Parisian mansion loaned by the millionaire Sao Schlumberger in March 1994. Galliano was patently anti-grunge and in October of the same year returned with a collection entitled *Pin Up* that had a very New Look style. A great fan of travelling back through time, the fashion agitator encapsulated the golden age of haute couture and adopted the artifices of 1950s fashion. 'Now more than ever it feels right to create clothes in a much more tailored and constructed way'[17] – a redesigned bust, an ultra-cinched waist, accentuated hips and a curved figure. The reference was purposefully explicit: 'It was my vision of Monsieur Dior,' confided Galliano in the pages of French *Vogue*. 'Of course, nobody at the time could have guessed what would come next, starting with myself.'[18] Given the impact this collection created, it seems obvious that it would stimulate ideas among the management of the House of Dior, which was looking for a new lease of life at the time.

Once Galliano joined Dior, he happily summoned up the 1950s and their imagery. For the Spring–Summer 2004 haute couture collection, for example, he exaggerated the female silhouette with a return to the famous *H* line launched by Christian Dior in 1954, which he mixed with lavish echoes of the pharaohs after a visit to Cairo, Luxor and Aswan, during which he noted that the long slender Egyptian statues looked much like the statuesque models of the 1950s. The models on the catwalk faced the line-up of photographers with their hands on their hips and their backs arched, imitating the numerous shots by Richard Avedon and Irving Penn, which Galliano compiled in his inspiration notebook for that season. Did he know that it was one of Avedon's shots of Marella Agnelli that inspired Christian Dior's *H* line?

These representations of an outrageously idealized beauty present a feast of looks that continue to inspire numerous designers and photographers today. 'Voguing' echoes the highly choreographed poses of the models who gave these images new life. 'I want heads, I want arms, I want legs!' snapped Diana Vreeland, the extravagant editor-in-chief of US *Vogue* from 1962 to 1971, after ripping out an overtly tame layout that had just been presented. 'I want feet! I want hands!'[19] Showing beautiful clothes was not enough – something had to actually happen in the shot. We want 'ladies with attitude', as Madonna sings in *Vogue*. Some photographers now call upon renowned choreographers to guide their models in front of the camera. Since 2001, Inez Van Lamsweerde and Vinoodh Matadin have been working with Stephen Galloway, the former principal dancer for the Frankfurt Ballet. 'It's like a very bizarre pas de trois,' Galloway says. 'It's about rhythm, this furious kind of breath and excitement, and it's never boring.'[20] The result is consistently surprising and shines a new light on the couturier's creations, as Christian Dior willingly acknowledged back in 1956: 'A detail which I had inserted without thinking, and which had become lost in the course of the execution of the dress, will emerge miraculously under the pencil of the artist or through the objective lens of the camera, as a result of a curious angle or unexpected lighting. Perhaps these revelations are a proof of the independence of my creations from their creator.'[21] Driven by a mutual love for beauty, this creator of beautiful images reveals different aspects of the designs to their original designer; he has the power to turn a dress designed for a single season into a form that defies time itself, destined to be everlasting.

Right **INEZ VAN LAMSWEERDE & VINOODH MATADIN** 2013
Pages 86–87 **WILLY VANDERPERRE** 2014

Above **CLIFFORD COFFIN** 1954
Right **DAVID SIMS** 2006

Above and right **GREG KADEL** 2007

Left **DAVID SIMS** 1997
Above **WILLIAM KLEIN** 1960

Above **CECIL BEATON** 1951
Right **PETER LINDBERGH** 1997
Pages 96–97 **NICK KNIGHT** 2011

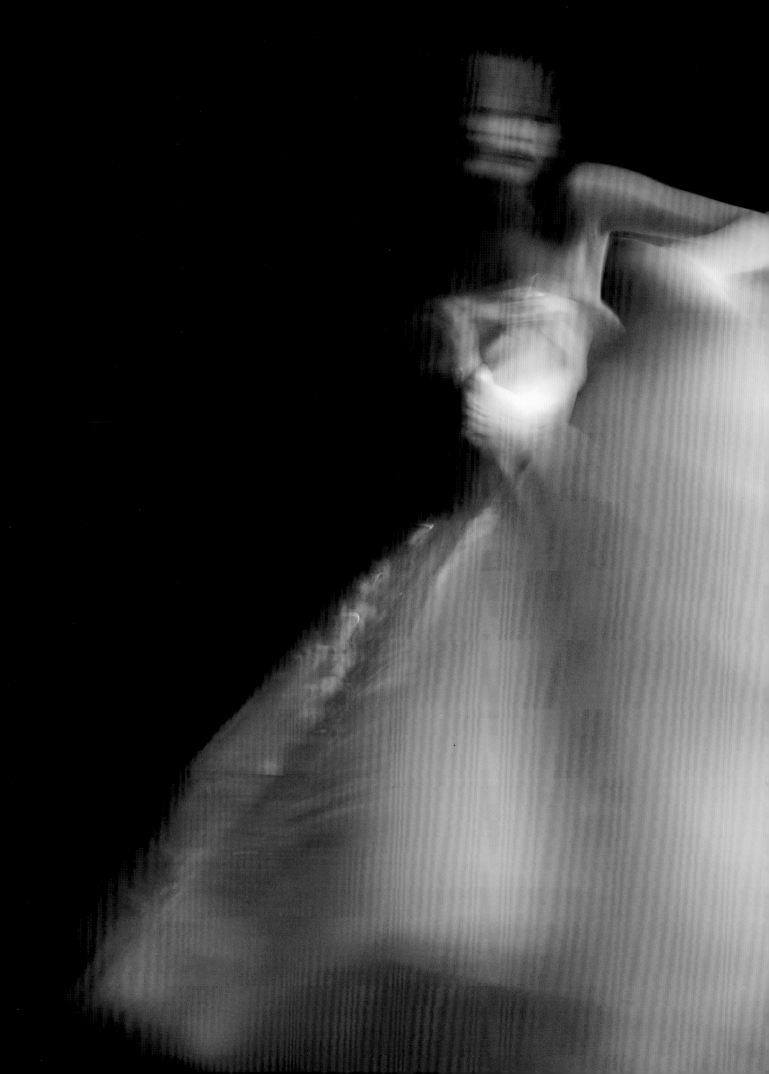

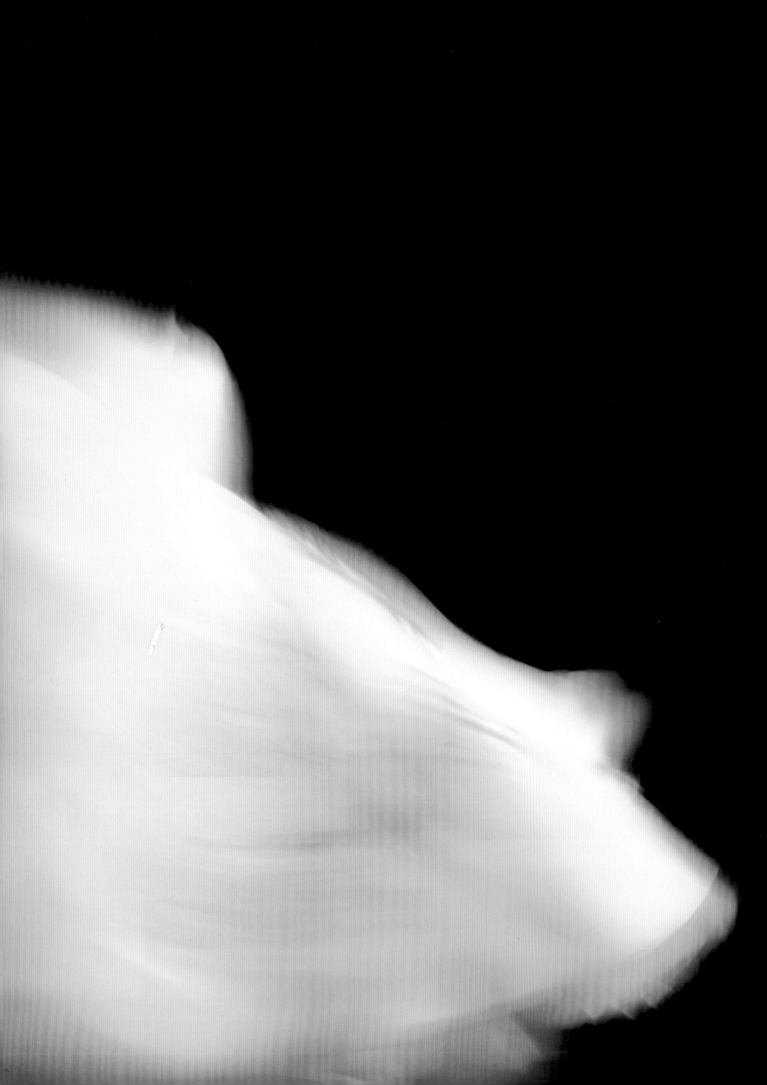

SNOWDON 1986

Above **LOUISE DAHL-WOLFE** 1955
Right **ALBERT WATSON** 1989

Left **HORST P. HORST** 1949
Above **INEZ VAN LAMSWEERDE** & **VINOODH MATADIN** 2013

Above **CLIFFORD COFFIN** 1948
Right **PATRICK DEMARCHELIER** 1991

Right **IRVING PENN** 1950
Pages 110–111 **WILLY VANDERPERRE** 2014

Return of Romance

In the aftermath of the war, a happy few awoke from a twilight world to revive a party lifestyle that was doomed to die out – but did they even know it at the time? The members of the Café Society microcosm lived for the moment and delighted in their new-found freedom in a deluge of revelling and amusement. Aristocrats, millionaires, men and women of letters, figures of the arts and fashion (couturiers, jewelers, journalists, photographers) got together in the evenings to enjoy the postwar whirl at an occasion that would let them fulfil their desire to shine: the grand society balls. From 1947, a constellation of society balls illuminated the nights of these privileged few. This resurgence of luxury and a certain *art de vivre* was a clear echo of the haute couture revival that the New Look had brought on that same year. 'The Maison Christian Dior profited from this wave of optimism and the return of an ideal of civilized happiness.'[1]

The festivities started in June with three balls a week – the fine weather providing a chance to catch up after an excessively harsh winter. There were debutante balls of course, such as the one held by Princess Elisabeth Chavchavadzé, who invited some 600 people into the gardens of her private mansion on Rue de Bellechasse in Paris to celebrate her daughter Hélène de Breteuil's coming out. The early summer ball that could not be missed, however, was the aptly named Bal du Panache, presided over by the British ambassador and his wife, Sir Alfred Duff Cooper and Lady Cooper, to raise funds for the Marie-Thérèse dispensary in Malakoff. The couple gave Christian Bérard carte blanche to organize a glittering event.

With his down-and-out airs and long scruffy beard, it was not outwardly easy to imagine the importance of the man known as 'Bébé Bérard', or simply 'Bébé'. Yet this jovial artist of many talents (painter, illustrator, costume and stage designer) was a prince of Parisian nights, a party-going 'arbiter of elegance', as his friend Christian Dior pointed out.[2] For the Bal du Panache, which truly inaugurated the postwar party era, the stage-master transformed the three grand salons of the Maison de L'Amérique Latine into a luxurious forest that enchanted the 2,000 guests. Bérard turned the ball into a work of art. 'Thanks to him,' *Vogue* Paris commented, 'we maintain the wonders of certain enchanted nights, the memory of which still haunts us.'[3]

Clad in feathers, flowers and butterflies and twinkling with tiaras, diadems and precious stones, the ladies played their part with suitable panache. 'For weeks,' observed

US *Vogue*, 'the dressmakers and modistes were busy designing special headdresses for the ball.'[4] On the polished mahogany parquet gleaming like a mirror, the *femmes-fleurs* bloomed with grace: here Christian Dior's *Corolle* line could truly flourish – how long it had been since anyone had seen such a grand demonstration of elegance. The order book for the House of Dior's sumptuous and extravagant gowns was full and balls were held in ever greater numbers. 'As if possessed by a frenzy, everybody wanted to give his ball for a particular work, or for his friends, in Paris, in the country, on the Eiffel Tower, on a boat on the Seine, anywhere where it was a novelty to dance', Christian Dior recalled.[5]

'Paris was looking its best, this summer of 1948,' said US *Vogue*. 'Little pasteboards, little blue telegrams of invitations, seemed to fall like rain.'[6] High society hastened to the Bal de la Rose, the Bal de la Voilette, the Bal du Ruban, the Pré Catalan and the Nuit de la Tour Eiffel, under which the Bouglione circus had mounted its big top for a special gala, followed by a dinner lit up by a gigantic firework display. The absolute climax of this *Grande Saison* was the carnival held by Antonio de Carvalho e Silva in July 1948. The 24-year-old Portuguese millionaire turned the Piscine Deligny into a midsummer night's palace for a Venetian ball. 'Surrounded with flowers, the swimming pool turned into a dream lake,' recalled Christian Dior, who must have been present given his detailed description of the event. 'The glow of the candles, and the ingenious Spanish Moroccan façades erected in wood, reminded me of the Palace of the Doges, while the guests in their dominoes, passing in and out of the airy arcades, were like the characters in a comic opera.'[7]

The winter was brightened by the Bal des Oiseaux. It was held in December 1948 by Princess Guy de Polignac and a number of her friends to raise money to rebuild two dispensaries in the 16th arrondissement of the capital that had been destroyed by the bombings. The party, resembling a painting by Watteau, was held in the Palais Rose, home to Anna Gould, Duchesse de Talleyrand, which the Baron de Cabrol had transformed into a luxurious aviary. Built on Avenue du Bois (today Avenue Foch) between 1896 and 1902 by Gould's ex-husband, Comte Boni de Castellane, the residence (which is no longer standing today) had been inspired by the Grand Trianon in Versailles. Dressed in the most exquisite haute couture, a flock of fabulous creatures concealed behind feathered masks waltzed beneath the chandeliers. Among the finest feathered friends were the Marquesa Ico Di Rende and the Comtesse de la Baume, both dressed in diaphanous gala gowns from Dior – they wore the models *Coquette* and *Eugénie* ('the most expensive dress in Paris') respectively.[8] Nothing was too beautiful for the occasion: the couturier used the most sumptuous fabrics and produced the fairy-tale effect that everyone was longing for. 'A ball gown is your dream, and it must make you a dream … And it is wonderful for morale.'[9]

Christian Dior, whose notoriety was growing with each and every collection, was firmly on the list of the society people to know. Although he was chronically shy and stayed

CECIL BEATON 1951

relatively discreet during the parties, he nonetheless accepted an invitation from Etienne de Beaumont, a count and wealthy heir of one of the grandest families in France. He was a major figure in Café Society, which made his mansion on Rue Masseran its epicentre. Since the early twentieth century, he and his wife Edith had organized exclusive soirées there for people of their standing and men and women of the arts, on just one condition: that they be brilliant and talented spirits. The couple were major patrons of the arts at the time, supporting Serge Diaghilev and the Ballets Russes, Jean Cocteau and Pablo Picasso, Georges Braque or Erik Satie and Darius Milhaud. Their parties had no match, most especially their spectacular, fantasy-laden costume balls. Etienne de Beaumont even served as the inspiration for Comte Anne d'Orgel, the hero of Raymond Badiguet's second novel, *Le Bal du comte d'Orgel*, published in 1924.

The aristocratic dandy had held countless balls in the period between the wars – his last coup de grâce had been the Bal du Tricentenaire de Racine on 30 June 1939 – but during the Occupation was obliged to dim the party lights. Now that Paris was liberated, he naturally wanted to revive the excitement of party life. In January 1949 he reopened his music room for a Bal des Rois et des Reines (kings and queens ball), held for his nephew Henri's entry into society. Christian Dior simply could not miss it because he knew the count very well: De Beaumont designed costume jewelry to go with the couturier's dresses. Dior also knew that their mutual friends would be in attendance – Christian Bérard and Leonor Fini. All he had left to do was find a costume that went with the theme: Dior would be the king . . . of animals, a lion. He asked Pierre Cardin to dress him. Cardin had recently left his post as a first tailor at the House of Dior on a whim, after a 'copying scandal' for which he was wrongly accused.[10] He had partnered with Marcel Escoffier to set up a stage-costume design business that could supply fancy dress for balls. Loyal and faithful to the end, Dior became his first client, as Cardin recounts: 'Pierre, to thank you for your presence in my couture house, I would like you to make my lion costume.'[11]

Pierre Cardin had started out with Paquin in 1944. Paquin and his creative director at the time, Antonio Castillo, were the designers chosen by Christian Bérard and Marcel Escoffier to make the costumes for the film *Beauty and the Beast*, directed by Jean Cocteau in 1945 and released the following year. Cardin had dreamed of being an actor or a dancer and threw himself wholeheartedly into the adventure – he even wore Jean Marais' costume to act as a body double for the action scenes.[12] The images of Dior arriving with regal poise, looking handsome yet troubling in his sumptuous animal-king costume, led one to believe that Cardin must have drawn on his experience for *Beauty and the Beast*. Dior wore a dashing dinner suit with a blue and gold scarf and a large red satin cummerbund, a ruff around his neck and a sceptre in hand. His embroidered tulle and taffeta cape and his mask – or rather headdress – were spectacular: a lion's head on his forehead (Dior's eyes were at the level of the lion's tongue, made of crimson silk velvet, which served as a mask).

Right THEO GRAHAM, EVENING GOWN BY DIOR, PRÉ CATALAN,
PARIS, AUGUST 1949. PHOTOGRAPH BY **RICHARD AVEDON**
Pages 122–23 **MARIO TESTINO** 2011

CLIFFORD COFFIN 1948

The couturier stood out among the eminent society figures around him: Princess Ghislaine de Polignac (dressed as Marie-Antoinette), Count Sforza (as the King of Nougat), Jacques and Geneviève Fath (as Charles IX and Queen Elisabeth of Austria, his wife), Elsa Schiaparelli (as Queen Bee), Leonor Fini (as Queen of the Underworld), Henri Sauguet (as one of the three wise men) and Christian Bérard (as Henry VIII) – the Bal des Rois would be the last ball that Bébé attended: he passed away on 12 February 1949.

Christian Dior would wear fancy dress again two years later at the grand gala held by Marie-Laure de Noailles on 16 January 1951, at 'Lune-sur-Mer, its beach, its casino, its forest, its curiosities'. With the help of Georges Geffroy and Alexis de Redé, the eccentric viscountess had transformed her flamboyant mansion on Place des Etats-Unis into an imaginary resort ready to receive a succession of quirky, burlesque characters. Dressed as a candy seller, she welcomed the American Ambassador David Bruce and his wife, disguised as a valet and chambermaid, the Baronne de Cabrol disguised as a woman with no legs, the Clifford sisters as flower bushes, Maxime de la Falaise as a weeping willow, Balthus as a Pierrot, Jean Dessès as a clown, Elsa Schiaparelli as a goat, Princess Chavchavadzé as a tobacconist, Marie-Louise Bousquet as a bistro owner, Comte Jacques de la Béraudière as a bartender, and Arturo López and Christian Dior as waiters. Café Society was definitely having a ball. At the last one he ever attended, held by his friend Marie-Laure de Noailles and themed 'To the glory of Painters and Writers from the 15th to the 20th centuries', Dior dressed as the writer Barbey d'Aurevilly, who hailed from Normandy like himself.

Among the high-society events of the 1950s, one ball outshone all the rest. In Spring 1951, a few hundred hand-picked souls in Europe and the United States had the privilege of receiving an invitation from Charles de Beistegui, requesting they do him 'the honour of spending the evening at home, at the Palazzo Labia in Venice, on September 3rd 1951 from 10.30 pm.' The heir to a phenomenal fortune (he was the grandson of silver mine owners in Mexico), Beistegui wanted to show off the palazzo he had purchased in 1948, on the corner of the Grand Canal and the Cannaregio Canal, having recently completed its restoration and interior decoration. Everybody wanted to be part of this extraordinary 'house-warming' party – the invitations had to be sent out in three different versions to guard against counterfeits. Far from the drudge of daily existence, the preparations got underway in an atmosphere of euphoria. They would last for several months.

One of the most highly anticipated guests was the Honourable Mrs Reginald Fellowes, known as 'Daisy' (thanks to her Christian name, Marguerite). She was the daughter of Duc Jean Decazes de Glücksberg and Isabelle Singer, the wealthy heiress of the inventor of Singer sewing machines. First married to Prince Jean de Broglie, Daisy was widowed in 1918 and a year later wed the banker Reginald Fellowes, a cousin of Winston Churchill. She had a name, beauty and a fortune – all the ingredients needed to join the Café Society and

become its queen during the period between the wars. She was a woman of incredible taste and self-confidence and was fearless about fashion: 'nothing was too extreme for Daisy', wrote Carmel Snow, who had seen her fair share of outlandish styles.[13] So much so that in the 1930s the editor-in-chief of *Harper's Bazaar* did not hesitate to hire this atypical collaborator, an aristocrat through her father and a millionaire through her mother.

At the Beistegui ball, this icon of the latest fashions decided to embody America in 1750. She was a regular haute couture client and ordered her costume from Christian Dior, who drew his inspiration from the tapestries hanging in the Palazzo Labia to create a yellow gala gown spiced up with leopard print. 'She wore a dress trimmed with leopard print, the first time we had seen such a thing (still fashionable today, sixty years on), and was attended by four young men painted the colour of mahogany,' Deborah Devonshire wrote in 2010.[14] A magnificent photograph shot by Cecil Beaton (who was dressed as an abbot) remains as a vestige of this grand evening; it shows Daisy Fellowes looking serious in front of Tiepolo's *The Banquet of Cleopatra*, followed by the architect James Caffery decked out as a servant, holding a pagoda-shaped parasol (see p. 117). Dior also dressed the star of *Beauty and the Beast*, the actress Josette Day, in a hoop dress with a plunging cleavage under a black wool coat with leopard-skin lapels.

Dior himself wore a large indoor coat in silver lamé with wide white satin borders – identical to the ones worn by his friends Salvador Dalí and Gala, Marie-Louise Bousquet and Victor Grandpierre. All wore masks and represented the ghosts of Venice. Dior and Dalí had got together to dream up their impressive 'Entrance of the Giants'. On one of the watercolours by Alexandre Serebriakoff, commissioned by Beistegui to record the highlights of the party for posterity, six giants stand around a man-sized creature in the middle of the ballroom. Designed by Dior and once again created by Pierre Cardin, their costumes were inspired by the *bauta* (domino), the hooded cape typically seen at the Venice Carnival.[15]

'It was the most incredible fancy-dress ball,' recalled Patricia López-Wilshaw, who regularly attended the most prestigious parties with her cousin and her husband Arturo.[16] The 'Masks and Dominoes' ball, as some called it, went down in history and left a lasting impression on its era. As the number of grand balls dwindled, it came to be known as the 'Ball of the Century'. It was the flamboyant brainchild of Charles de Beistegui, the leading light of a declining Café Society, dreamed up to ward off the dull reality of normal life. 'Parties like that are genuine works of art,' wrote Christian Dior: 'people may be annoyed by them, by the very fact that they are on a grand scale – nevertheless they are desirable, and important even in the history of our time, because they produce the authentic sense of popular enjoyment.'[17]

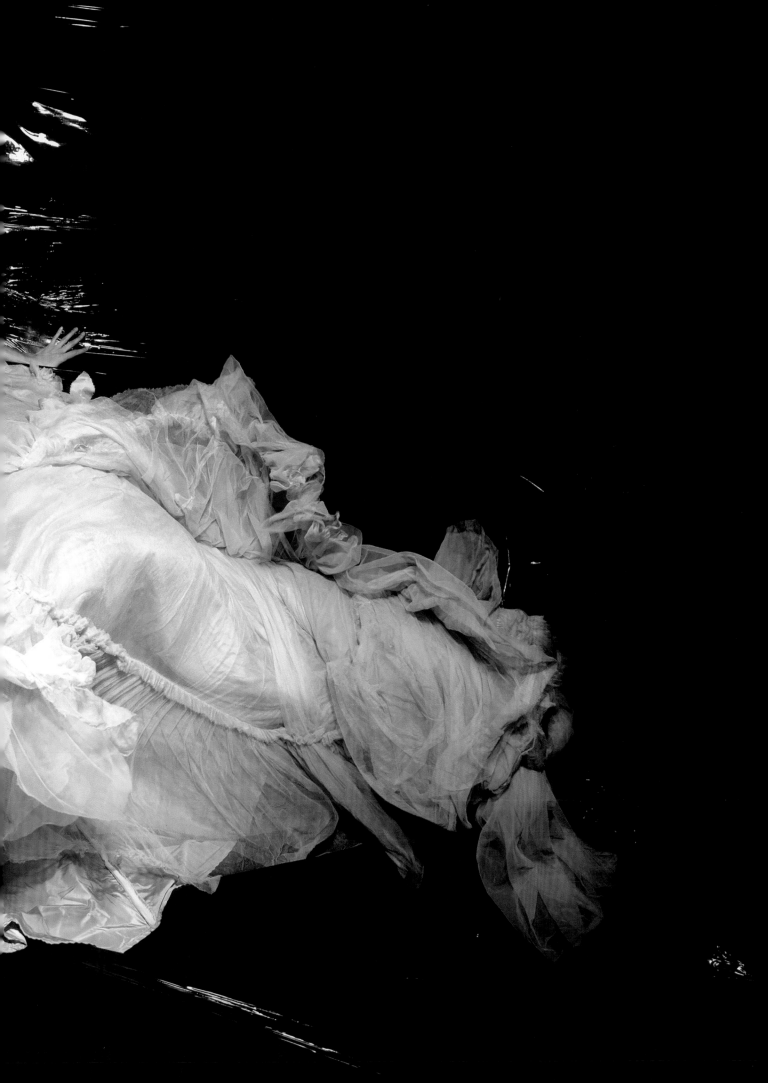

Pages 136–37 RIHANNA **STEVEN KLEIN** 2015
Left **CLIFFORD COFFIN** 1948
Pages 140–41 DAFT PUNK **PETER LINDBERGH** 2013

139

Christian Dior was a level-headed man who wore such classical clothes, but who expressed his sense of enchantment through his love of fancy dress, which he nurtured from an early age back in Granville: 'I could be amused for hours by anything that was sparkling, elaborate, flowery, or frivolous.'[18] When Dior was growing up he actively participated in the children's parties and the Zigotto-Circus, a parody that involved parents and children, as well as the inevitable Carnival des Fleurs (Flower Carnival), which was the main attraction of the summer season. They all provided occasions for him to dream up new costumes for himself and his friends – his very first creations. He designed a costume for Suzanne Luling, who went on to become the director of his haute couture salons many years later. In her diary she recalls: 'at the end of the letter which accompanied the sketch, he added this note: "The skirt is longer at the back. Hold the skirt up a little with the hand."'[19] Though Dior had no idea he would work in fashion one day, he already demonstrated a clear sense of the art of dressing up.

As a young man in Paris, he made new friends with whom he loved to go out and have fun. They were the musician Henri Sauguet, the poet Max Jacob and the painter Christian Bérard. 'To the music of a gramophone, Max, who seemed youngest of us all, would discard his slippers and dance in red stockings, mimicking a whole corps de ballet to Chopin's *Préludes*. Sauguet and Bérard, helped by lampshades, counterpanes, and curtains, would turn themselves into all the characters of history. It was my part in those first charades and those games with historical costumes at the hôtel Nollet [where Max Jacob lived at the time]... That wonderful time when our youth ran free, the year 1928, a millennium in my eyes'.[20] Christian Dior was twenty-three years old and it would be a long while before he partied again. After living a happy-go-lucky, dilettante lifestyle, he would traverse a series of misfortunes: his father's bankruptcy, the outbreak of war in Europe and the deportation of his sister. Dior flew in the face of adversity, however, meeting his destiny as a couturier much later in life. He would spend the rest of his days turning ordinary reality into something wonderful. In this, he was helped by the mood that prevailed at the time.

After the war, people were seeking light-heartedness again and parties proved to be a powerful remedy to the pain they had suffered. Just as World War I gave rise to the Roaring Twenties, merriment resurfaced with the return of economic growth after World War II. The fashions, however, were different: the 1920s bore witness to a modernist drive, with women sporting short bob hairstyles and shirt-dresses, dancing the Charleston to jazzy rhythms in clubs with Art Deco designs. The late 1940s, however, were ripe with nostalgia. If the long twirling skirts, wasp waists and full busts presented by Christian Dior in 1947 seem to contradict the very meaning of the term 'new look', it is because this apparently modern expression drew its roots from throwbacks to the past. The inaugural *Corolle* and *En 8* lines exude an aura of memory, reminders of a glorified Belle Epoque. The New Look nostalgia caused a revolution; contrary to all expectations it grew popular and reached its climax in the mid-twentieth century.

Just as the half-century was being fêted, a number of films were released whose plots recalled the pre-war days: *Occupe-toi d'Amélie*, *Miquette et sa mère*, *Véronique* and *Le Roi*. In Paris, the Théâtre Antoine performed *Le Petit Café*, Tristan Bernard's hit play from 1911. On screen and on stage, French stars walked 'with dainty steps': Danielle Darrieux, Danielle Delorme, Gisèle Pascale and Annie Ducaux appeared with guipure collars, leg-of-mutton sleeves, puffs, flounces and frills around figure-hugging corsets. Songs too harked back to the past: the café-concert ditties of Yvette Guilbert, the lovestruck ballads of Paul Delmet, the songs and poems of Aristide Bruant . . . Maurice Chevalier released 'Paris 1900' and a host of artists recorded timeless songs such as 'Bonsoir Madame la Lune', 'En r'venant d'la revue', 'Le Petit Coeur de Ninon' or 'Frou-Frou'. In the late 1940s, nobody was dreaming of the bleak modernity of the 1920s: 'Abundance was still much too much of a novelty for a poverty cult to develop out of inverted snobbism', wrote Christian Dior.[21] He was right to bring back the refined silhouettes of his mother's day, delighting contemporary ladies who were ready to be seduced by a Belle Epoque style that flaunted its frivolity. Fashion delved into the annals of its past: 1950 harked back to 1900, whose inspiration came from the Second Empire, which had borrowed from the eighteenth century.

In 1949, the director Marcel Achard, who was well aware of the New Look's nods to the past, asked Christian Dior to design twenty-two outfits for Yvonne Printemps, the actress who was due to play Hortense Schneider, a diva from Napoleon III's reign, in the film *La Valse de Paris*. Dior's twenty-two gowns revived the highly sophisticated fashion of Empress Eugénie, Napoleon III's wife, who loved fashion so much her critics nicknamed her the 'clothes fairy'. The beauty, wealth and power of France had to be flaunted before the other courts of Europe, and this naturally involved prestigious dress. Eugénie did nothing to hide her fascination for a former French queen, Marie-Antoinette, whose style she echoed. Not only did Eugénie bring the pastel pinks, yellows and violets of the 1770s back into fashion, she also decided to widen the circumference of her skirts and was extremely fond of crinoline, recalling hoop dresses and farthingales. In lieu of the layers of heavy skirts piled over whalebone frames, in 1856 a more supple and lightweight structure was invented to produce the desired volume. Crinolines would grow fuller and wider until Charles Frederick Worth, the Paris-based English couturier who was a favourite of Eugénie, replaced these unwieldy cages with more manageable bustles.

Eugénie displayed the same obsessive fascination for Marie-Antoinette in the field of interiors as well. The Second Empire style was characterized by an eclectic synthesis of the best of other period styles and brought back a penchant for late eighteenth-century furniture, which returned to fashion again in the early twentieth century and formed the

décor for the Dior family apartment in Paris in 1910. 'It was there that I discovered and was conquered for ever by "Louis Seize-Passy" with its white-enamelling, doors with little bevel-edged panels, many window-flounces, macramé net curtains, panels of cretonne or damask depending on the degree of luxury of the room, interspaced with rococo flowers thought to be "Pompadour" but which were in fact already "Vuillard".[22] With its white and Trianon-grey *médaillon* chairs, woodwork, mouldings and pendant chandeliers, the Louis XVI style would go on to play an essential part in the visual identity of the couture house and its boutiques, starting with the flagship on Avenue Montaigne.

Christian Dior contemplated the Enlightenment and drew inspiration from the classical French repertory. 'Dior is a magnificent painting that you hang on the wall,' noted Yves Saint Laurent. 'Dior is ornament, pomp and construction ... Baroque construction.'[23] From Regency to Louis XVI, the couturier's fondness for the eighteenth century is clearly apparent in the imaginary realm from which he took the names for his creations: *Pompadour*,[24] *Du Barry*,[25] *Nattier, Watteau* and *Fragonard*,[26] *Versailles*,[27] *Fête à Versailles*,[28] *Trianon*,[29] *Bal à Trianon*,[30] *Bal d'autrefois*,[31] *Bal de Cour*[32] and *Bal Romantique*,[33] *Fête galante*.[34] A look at the collection charts – precious documents preserved in the House of Dior archives that list each silhouette for each season (name, sketch, identity of the première d'atelier who supervised it and of the model who presented it, along with samples of the fabrics used) – shows one name that crops up several times: *Grand Mogol* (or simply *Mogol*).[35] 'Au Grand Mogol' was the name of a shop on Rue Saint Honoré, near the Palais Royal, opened in 1773 by Marie-Jeanne Bertin, a young woman from Picardy with an imagination as awesome as her ambition. She moved to Paris to become one of the most famous fashion tradeswomen in the French kingdom and the royal courts of its neighbours, working under the name Rose Bertin. She owed her prestige to Marie-Antoinette, to whom she was introduced on 11 May 1774 – the day after Louis XV's death, therefore the first day the young Austrian princess became queen   by the Duchesse de Chartres, whose wedding gown she had created five years earlier.

Marie-Antoinette was eighteen years old and the Court of Versailles bored her; Rose Bertin brought her the touch of fantasy she needed and satisfied her fashion follies. The Queen would retire for hours with her 'minister of fashions' in her private apartments, trying on the latest creations before ordering great quantities in a frenzy. Tall, slim and well proportioned, the Queen wore Bertin's creations beautifully and was largely responsible for boosting the latter's success. Au Grand Mogol supplied the other members of the royal family, such as the Comtesse de Provence, the Comtesse d'Artois and Madame Elisabeth (Louis XVI's sister), the Queens of Sweden, Spain and Bohemia, the Princesse Palatine des Deux-Ponts and the Grand-Duchess of Russia, as well as actresses, dancers, intellectuals and artists, and even Marie-Antoinette's sworn enemy, the Comtesse du Barry.

Left **DAVID SEIDNER** 1992
Above **LILLIAN BASSMAN** 1949

Their custom meant Rose Bertin was in high demand – she did not sew and was therefore not a couturier in the literal sense of the term. She laid the foundations for what Worth would turn into haute couture over a century later: seasonal collections of new styles conceived by a designer. According to Christian Dior, Rose Bertin invented fashion in the modern sense of the term.[36]

Dior drew inspiration from Marie-Antoinette and Rose Bertin for the fashion repertoire that he offered the elegant ladies of his time. The press kit detailing the Spring–Summer 1955 collection reads: 'for the evening and the most formal circumstances, we have borrowed the most delicate colours from preciously preserved samples in the wardrobe of the most touching, the most elegant of our queens: Marie-Antoinette blue, "Bertin" pink, Versailles white and gold, Trianon grey, Dauphin green, "Queen's Hair" blonds and Royal red.'[37]

References to the eighteenth century sometimes appeared in a more unexpected context. In the Spring–Summer 1952 collection, 'a lacquer chest of drawers from the Louis XV period was the starting point for three dresses, red, black and white, executed with the perfection of the most prestigious embroideries from the olden days.'[38] For Autumn–Winter 1957 (Dior's final collection), the late afternoon dresses again took on a style inspired by the *fête galante* paintings of Fragonard, Watteau and Nattier: comely cleavages, tight busts, puffy silk skirts and underskirts, velvet ottomans and sumptuous brooches, all adorned with bows, roses, ribbons and romantic flounces. Lush embroideries covered full dresses in pastel shades, worthy of the finest courtly outfits. 'Girls could safely feel that they had all the trappings of a fairy-tale princess to wear.'[39]

For footwear, Christian Dior called upon the best shoemakers in the world, first André Perugia and Salvatore Ferragamo, then Roger Vivier. Dior and Vivier met in 1947, but only truly started to work together from 1953 – Vivier was the only person allowed to place his name alongside the Dior signature ('Christian Dior crée par Roger Vivier' could be read on the Louis XVI-style label inside the shoes and on the shoe boxes from 1958). The couturier had found the ideal craftsman to combine excellence and fantasy in a shoe – at Dior, the more elegant term 'soulier' (slipper or footwear) was always used instead of 'chaussure' (shoe): 'Can you imagine talking about Marie-Antoinette's "shoes"?' the couturier enquired of Vivier one day.[40] Like Dior, Vivier was very much inspired by the eighteenth century, which moved him to create the most delicate models. As the height of refinement, he made the footwear match the dresses – crafted from the same precious, fragile fabrics and studded with gems, pendants, spangles and sequins, generally embroidered by the great René Bégué, known as 'Rébé' – a master of fancy adornment whose reputation was forged through this collaboration. Vivier reinvented the Louis XV slanting heel, which he then rendered even more slender (the beginnings of his 'comma' heel).

Pages 152–53 **TIM WALKER** 2004
Pages 154–55 **PAOLO ROVERSI** 1997
Left **NORMAN PARKINSON** 1950

Left **LOUISE DAHL-WOLFE** 1947
Above **TIM WALKER** 2012

Above **HENRY CLARKE** 1952
Right **JUERGEN TELLER** 1999

Vivier also developed the stiletto heel in 1954, which he slanted progressively inwards towards the sole of the foot. With heels that defied the laws of gravity and tips as pointy as 'bird beaks', Vivier's haute couture shoes were not the easiest items to wear (the 'princesses' often needed to have feet as slender as Cinderella's), but every elegant woman simply had to own a pair. Queen Elizabeth, who wore Vivier shoes for her coronation, the Duchess of Windsor, Marlene Dietrich, Elizabeth Taylor, Sophia Loren and the Shahbanu Farah Diba feature among the most famous clients past and present.

In 1958, the year after Christian Dior's death, Vivier renewed his contract for five years. He invented increasingly innovative forms that often drew on references from the eighteenth century to accompany creations by Yves Saint Laurent and then Marc Bohan. Dior's two successors were guardians of the house tradition, but as the postwar boom period progressed, they gradually broke away from the eighteenth-century influence. Bohan, who was creative director from the early 1960s through to 1989, cultivated a style that was quite different to Christian Dior's notion of fashion – though he must simply have been following the mood of the moment. Lavishness made way for a certain sense of moderation, in terms of effect rather than means. 'I above all sought to make very contemporary clothes,' wrote Dior, 'a complete fashion for today's life, and not reveries of things past.'[41] Not until the arrival of Gianfranco Ferré, who presented his first collection in July 1989, was the rustle of precious flowing gala gowns heard again, striking symbols of an opulent haute couture. The fullness of grand ball gowns may have seemed surprising at the dawn of the 1990s – a time when grunge and minimalism triumphed – but they have nonetheless crossed the ages, in defiance against time.

'Defiance' is not a word that ever fazed John Galliano, the flamboyant troublemaker who defied all odds when he was appointed creative director of two gems of French couture owned by the LVMH group: Givenchy in 1995, then Dior in 1996. 'Surprised and thrilled. I didn't hesitate,' he confessed. 'I have dreamed of creating haute couture, it's the opportunity of a lifetime!'[42] As soon as he joined the house that launched the New Look half a century beforehand, Galliano combined his tailoring mastery with the unique savoir-faire of the *Tailleur* and *Flou* ateliers to produce his romantic vision of fashion and its history, all with erudite ease. Like Christian Dior, Galliano ranked dreams above everything else. Like Dior, he believed in memory and was passionate about the eighteenth century. 'It's true, the eighteenth century is an obsession of mine. But I reinterpret it, with corsets that are barely suggested, poetic hairstyles, sophisticated trains'.[43] Drawing more from films such as *Dear Caroline* and *Angélique* than from historical truth, he upheld the myth and the dreams, making them 'Galliano' and 'Diorissimo' at one and the same time.

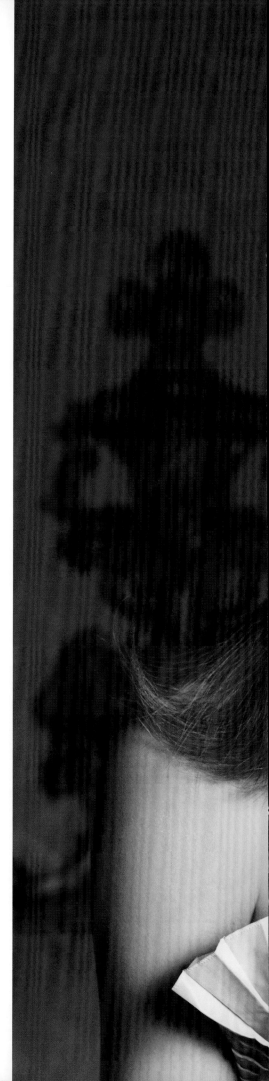

INEZ VAN LAMSWEERDE & VINOODH MATADIN 2006

Above **HORST P. HORST** 1979
Right **PAOLO ROVERSI** 2014

CLIFFORD COFFIN 1954

Under Victoire de Castellane, Dior jewelry too has taken a leaf out of couture's book and seen things in grand – if not oversize – style. After learning the ropes at Chanel, where she reinvented costume jewelry for fourteen years, the designer joined Dior in 1998 and combined the worlds of jewelry and fashion with humour and originality, revisiting the fairy-tale Dior world with delight. Playing on the established codes of the Place Vendôme, she debunked the sacred aura of jewels. She treated the most precious gemstones in a freestyle yet very 'couture' spirit, with diamonds, rubies, emeralds or sapphires inlaid on motifs of lace, ribbons, corset laces, feathers and pompoms – materials that were in high demand in eighteenth-century fashion boutiques. In a final homage to this dreamy era, jewelry was delicately tied in a bow at the back of the neck.

'Clothes need to be wearable. Nobody feels at ease with a train weighing 35 kilos', says Raf Simons.[44] The former industrial designer came with a reputation for being radical and minimalist, more passionate about Bauhaus architecture than neoclassicism: how was he going to be able to make Dior's beloved eighteenth-century romanticism his own and find an echo with today's world? 'I started by asking myself: "what is modernity?" I wanted to use a language that would be the exact opposite of the one I had used at Dior up until now,' said Simons of his Autumn–Winter 2014 haute couture collection. 'It struck me as more contemporary to move towards a far-off past rather than to modernize the spirit of the last decades. The challenge was to take a contemporary attitude towards something very historic, to bring simplicity and a casual style to something that could seem theatrical.'[45]

Rococo aesthetics and the rigidness of court dress no longer bear any relation to the modern world. 'I like what is clean, ordered and neat. I don't like powdery fashions and fabrics that are dusty . . . thick, stiff and stand on their own. I want them to move.'[46] Raf Simons nonetheless kept the charming sway of the panniers that underpinned French dresses in Louis XV's day, but using a tulle structure to make them totally light. A milky colour palette, ankle-length cuts, ethereal corsets and rounded necks, swimsuit-back armholes, zips and pockets: here French-style clothing reverted to a leotard (a man's jacket, long and narrow, always worn open) moulded onto a woman's body. Richly embroidered, it sufficed in itself – rejecting the historical reference, the designer felt no need to add anything: a sweater and black wool trousers would suit perfectly. Simons's neoromantic heroines walked confidently and serene, hands casually in their pockets. 'This is what allure is, in my opinion, this chic, relaxed side that emanates from a liberated woman.'[47] For Dior, Raf Simons reread history, transporting the house into a different space-time odyssey. 'The way the future uses the past is an idea I find fascinating.'[48]

EVENING SLIPPER, DESIGNED BY
ROGER VIVIER FOR DIOR, PARIS, AUGUST 1963.
PHOTOGRAPH BY **RICHARD AVEDON**

Right **DOMINIQUE ISSERMANN** 1992
Pages 180–81 **ELLEN VON UNWERTH** 1997

Right **TOM ORDOYNO** 2014
Pages 184–85 **PAOLO ROVERSI** 2014

Princesses in Bloom

On 21 August 1951, Princess Margaret celebrated her twenty-first birthday. To dance under the marquee in the grounds of Balmoral castle, the ideal setting for a romantic evening, she needed a gown fit for a princess. She chose a gown from Dior – a special creation, inspired by a model from the Spring–Summer 1951 haute couture collection: a short evening gown in white organza called *Matinée poétique*, embroidered with crystal, straw and mother-of-pearl. The Princess liked the delicately cinched corsage, the softly draped fabric of the bodice, which covered the left shoulder leaving the right shoulder bare, and the embroideries: 'I like it because it's got bits of potato peel on it', she said to her portraitist, Cecil Beaton.[1] The Princess nonetheless asked for the organza that formed the *décolleté* to wrap around her right arm and for the dress to be lengthened. *Matinée poétique* was calf-length – Margaret's ball gown would be long to suit her royal status and to evoke the fairy-tale image that she and the whole world expected.

There were no photographs of this special event. The official images immortalizing the youngest Windsor's coming of age in her haute couture gown were taken at Buckingham Palace a month earlier by Cecil Beaton. The doyen of British fashion photographers, whose work illustrated the pages of *Vogue*, knew Margaret well; he photographed her for the first time in 1942 when she was just twelve years old.

Cecil Beaton had started shooting portraits of the Royal Family in 1930, first at the request of Princess Louise, the daughter of Queen Victoria, then at the request of Prince George, the future Duke of Kent, and his sister-in-law, Lady Alice Montagu-Douglas-Scott, who would become the Duchess of Gloucester. He also had Wallis Simpson pose for a photograph he published in *Vogue*.[2] It was at Simpson's home in London that Beaton met the Prince of Wales, the future King Edward VIII. The couple very naturally asked him to photograph their wedding at the Château de Candé (Indre-et-Loire) in 1937. Given the scandalous nature of their union, condemned by the House of Windsor, the pictures could potentially have had Beaton blacklisted. Yet the new Queen Elizabeth chose him as the court photographer, surprising everyone in the process. After the shock of Edward VIII's abdication, the monarchy needed to restore its prestige by presenting an ideal image that would be devised by Beaton.

In 1938 Beaton had a second sitting with Princess Marina, the Duchess of Kent. She chose to wear Greek national dress (she was born Princess Marina of Greece and Denmark) and her official dress; he decided to photograph her in a floral setting and used an enlarged and inverted detail of his favourite painting as a backdrop: *The Swing* by Jean-Honoré Fragonard.[3] The series, executed 'in the manner of a painting by Winterhalter' in her own words, pleased Marina of Kent's sister-in-law, Queen Elizabeth, who summoned Beaton and appointed him official photographer at Buckingham Palace. Their first session took place in July 1939 in the Palace gardens in the late afternoon. But as soon as World War II broke out, these fairy-tale images would be put away. During the war, the King, the Queen and their two daughters portrayed themselves as a typical English family, shutting away their fabulous regalia and jewels and opting for deliberately ordinary clothes. This change did not suit Beaton, who was eager for glamour, nor one particular member of the Royal Family, who found it hard to comply with this new austerity: Princess Margaret.

'Ever since she was a girl, Margaret enjoyed drawing elegant ladies, slim and beautifully dressed', recalls her governess, Marion Crawford.[4] Coquette from an early age, Margaret rebelled when told she had a duty to wear clothes cut from her mother's old dresses and threw a tantrum whenever she had to wear a dress that looked like her sister's. 'Margaret has an innate dress sense,' Miss Crawford continued. 'She knows what suits her and has always stubbornly refused to be charmed by the pastel blues and pinks found all around the palace.'[5] She wanted to be like her aunt, Marina of Kent, one of the most elegant ladies in Europe and a favourite model of Beaton's: 'When I grow up I'm going to dress like Aunt Marina,' she told her governess one day.[6]

On 24 October 1942 Princess Elizabeth and Princess Margaret posed for Beaton for the very first time. He created a romantic pictorial portrait of the two princesses by placing them in front of the reproduction of Fragonard's *Le Petit Parc*, just like Molly and Peggy, the daughters of Thomas Gainsborough, who depicted them this way in one of his paintings.[7] Beaton was also an artist and an illustrator and composed his photographs like paintings, specifically in the style of works by Franz Xaver Winterhalter and Thomas Gainsborough, perfectly following the lineage of court portraits. Beaton transposed the neo-rococo style into photography, beautifying the setting and heightening the nobility of his model, enhancing the royalty's prestige like a modern-day Winterhalter. The German painter had been the official portraitist for European high society during the last thirty years of the nineteenth century: he knew how to transcend the beauty and grace of Queen Victoria, Empress Elisabeth of Austria (the famous Sissi) and Empress Eugénie, all shining in their shimmering gowns. Beaton became his spiritual heir, arriving at exactly the right time, as testified in the pictures of Princess Elizabeth and Princess Margaret, taken in March 1945 and published once peace had returned to Europe. The elements that Beaton captured in photography would be captured in fashion by one of his very good friends, a man whom he dubbed the 'Watteau of contemporary dressmakers': Christian Dior.[8]

Above **CECIL BEATON** 1951
Right **TYRONE LEBON** 2014
Pages 192–93 **JUERGEN TELLER** 1994

The New Look represented a return to a world of dreams that Europe, and European women in particular, were eager to make the most of. With the end of the war, people wanted to see an end to austerity and hardship. Presented in early 1947, Dior's first collection was a symbol: it represented the new elegance, a world of luxury, plenty and beauty. Freedom was back. The New Look spread across the world, starting in France and moving to America and the United Kingdom. Across the Channel, a young woman would become its unofficial, then official spokesperson. On 10 February 1948, Princess Margaret appeared dressed in an ordinary-looking coat that fell just above her knee. A month later she appeared wearing the same coat, but now lengthened; a band of fabric had been added so that the coat would reach mid-calf: the length that had been launched by Dior. 'Princess Margaret adopts the New Look "on a budget",' quipped *Elle* magazine.[9] Margaret had to dress within the limits of the allowance she received from her father and she had to be smart to keep up with the fashions, just like most of her peers.

It was Margaret who made the New Look popular in Great Britain. This was a godsend for the up-and-coming House of Dior, since the princess was extremely famous. The press had started to take an interest in her since the wedding of her sister Elizabeth and photographers chased her everywhere. Margaret would never be queen, but for the people she was the princess who managed to strike the ideal balance between age-old traditions and modern-day ideas, between Royal Highness and little Miss Ordinary.

The style of this avant-garde princess obviously had an effect on her clothes: thousands of women sought to copy her and fashion houses around the world kept abreast of what she was wearing. Her choice of dress had repercussions throughout the British textile industry and in America as well: copies of her dresses could be seen in the department stores on New York's Fifth Avenue, with notices that read: 'Princess Meg's model'. Although Margaret clearly displayed her liking for the New Look, she did not dress at Dior. It would not have been 'proper'. Be that as it may, Margaret wanted a 'grand' haute couture gown from Dior and she would get it – though she had to wait for a year.

'*Vive Margaret! Vive Margaret!*' On 28 May 1949 Parisians cheered Princess Margaret's arrival at the Gare de Lyon. She had been travelling through Italy and Switzerland and was due to spend four days in France before returning home. Her itinerary read like a series of postcards: Fontainebleau forest; lunch at a famous inn at Barbizon; Versailles and its Grandes Eaux fountain display (as well as the Petit Trianon and the Hameau de la Reine); dinner at Lapérouse on Quai des Grands Augustins; Montmartre and the Sacré Coeur, then Pigalle by night (she went dancing in a cabaret on Rue Blanche). She would not be completely delighted, however, until she saw Parisian fashion – especially the two couture houses that she found most exciting: Jean Dessès (who dressed her aunt, the Duchess of Kent) and Christian Dior.

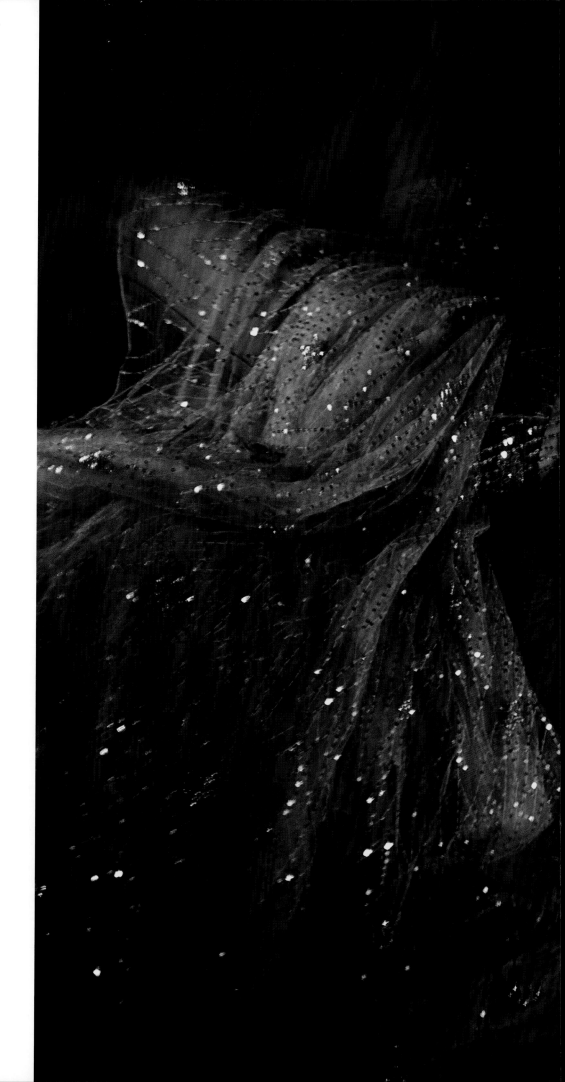

On 31 May the Princess attended a private presentation of the Spring–Summer 1949 collection in the grand salon at the House of Dior on Avenue Montaigne. There she could inspect the 170 models of Dior's *Trompe l'Oeil* line at close quarters. Although she liked the *Place Blanche* dress in Russian ermine and *Marly*, a gala ball gown in buttercup yellow faille, she left without passing any orders, obliged as she was to wear garments made in England: in accordance with court protocol, it was Norman Hartnell who designed her dresses for the official ceremonies.[10] Cleverly enough, the young woman managed to win her mother over. A few weeks later, Margaret's private secretary requested the House of Dior send over sketches of evening gowns. Three were sent to Buckingham Palace and Margaret chose the one that combined two of the emblematic models in the *Milieu de siècle* line from the Autumn–Winter 1949 collection: *Phalène*, a grand gala ball gown with a strapless bustier top, and the *Fidélité* wedding dress, with a white tulle crinoline skirt over which a large white satin sash was draped, then tied in a bow at the back, looking much like the models in Winterhalter's paintings.[11] The dress was approved of by the Queen and Margaret was given permission to place the order.

In order to ensure proper relations with a minimum number of fittings, Christian Dior hired a young woman with a buxom bust and a tiny waist, who had the same measurements as the princess. Nineteen-year-old Ghislaine de Boisson was a young woman from good stock who had resigned herself to abandoning her dreams of working as a model due to her small frame: to her great surprise she now joined the prestigious Dior *cabine*. 'I am very proud of being the first French mannequin to model a dress for the Royal Family', she declared a few months later, once her identity was revealed to the press.[12]

Accompanied by Mademoiselle Vere, an haute couture saleswoman, and a première main from the *Flou* atelier, the dress was flown to London. The fitting took place at Buckingham Palace in the Princess's bedroom, in the presence of Miss Jennifer Bevan, her lady's maid. Margaret always tried her dresses on at home so that she could study them when she moved. She practised sitting down in front of her white wardrobe with its trio of mirrors. 'The dress is difficult to manage,' Ghislaine de Boisson confided. 'It has so much whalebone I could hardly breathe and it has a big hoop around the hips, so the only way the princess can sit down in it is to slide the hoop over and squeeze on to about half a chair.'[13]

A few adjustments were made and the dress was delivered in a special trunk. It was everything the Princess had hoped for. The skirt was full and floating, made from 20 metres of white tulle; the white satin sash tied in a bow at the back was 5 metres long. The bodice was supposed to be strapless, but the Queen objected: 'It's very pretty but not proper enough; she will need a little shawl to cover the shoulders.' Dior obliged and added a small shawl.

The Princess was so pleased with her new dress that she could not wait for an official ceremony to wear it, putting it on for a private family dinner. 'My favourite dress of all was never photographed,' Margaret remembered many years later. 'It was my first Dior dress, white strapless tulle and a vast satin bow at the back.'[14] Little did she know that the dress had indeed been photographed by Henry Clarke for *L'Album du Figaro* (published in 1949), when it was worn not by the Princess but by her 'double', Ghislaine de Boisson. The magazine did not reveal the gown's true owner, of course. It had to wait for the official announcement on 14 November 1949, which left the London couture houses at a loss: how could Princess Margaret of the United Kingdom buy a 'French' dress? The young Royal Highness disregarded the critics and started what would be a highly privileged relationship with Christian Dior and his couture house.

The House of Dior informed its esteemed clients that 'due to a special presentation in London, its collection will not be presented on 25 and 26 April 1950.'[15] What was special about this presentation? Its audience: the Queen and her daughter, Princess Margaret. At 10 am on Wednesday 26 April 1950, a fleet of taxis picked up the mannequins Marie-Thérèse, Tania, France, Alla, Simone, Jane, Caroline and Sylvie from the Savoy, to take them to the French Embassy. Christian Dior was staying at Claridge's and met his 'girls' in the room that had been set aside as a dressing room to reveal the secret behind this mysterious presentation: 'You are going to present the collection to the Queen and Princess Margaret.'[16] They arrived in the company of Marina, the Duchess of Kent, her sister Princess Olga of Yugoslavia and several ladies of the court. Dior gave his models his final recommendations: their dresses did not enable them to curtsey, so they made do with a small bow to the Queen and the Princess, then exited through a door on the other side of the room, sidling along like crabs to ensure they never turned their backs to the Queen.

The names of the dresses were announced in French and the corresponding model number in English. The Queen and Princess Margaret asked the models for information about the dresses and the amount of fabric that they involved. Margaret noted down her favourite outfits. Dior made a few appearances but spent most of his time pacing nervously in a small antechamber, which the models went through to enter the salon. They presented the evening gowns last, this time each curtseying fully to the Queen, who congratulated them and asked to see the furs again, including two mink coats presented by Marie-Thérèse, who was flushed with pride and embarrassment. When the time came to leave, Margaret kindly extended her hand and, despite her surprise, Dior's star model executed a perfect curtsey.

The following year, to celebrate her twenty-first birthday, Margaret ordered a dress that has since become famous. It was photographed by Cecil Beaton in the Chinese sitting room at Buckingham Palace, which was transformed into a photo studio for the occasion.

The Princess wore little make-up, her pale, creamy complexion illuminated by a touch of bright lipstick and a dash of eyeliner. She had her hair styled in the usual way, her dark brown locks rolled into curls. Wreathed in romanticism in her idyllic ball gown, she posed standing, her hands crossed, flanked by hydrangeas and delphiniums, in front of the cascade of greenery in the gardens of the Villa d'Este painted by Fragonard in *Le Petit Parc*. It was Beaton's favourite painting. The portrait was inspired by Winterhalter, once again suggesting the hidden charm of royal courts of old, and is one of the most lyrical photographs of Princess Margaret ever taken (p. 202). Beaton also photographed her seated in a pink room on a padded sofa upholstered in purple silk, the walls adorned with tapestries illustrating the life of Don Quixote by François Boucher (p. 186). 'The princess looked so small in front of my camera,' the photographer recalled. 'Through the lens I could see her wonderful complexion, the fresh pink of her cheeks, the deep blue of her feline eyes. She wore a Dior dress that she was very proud of.'[17] This photograph of Margaret taken by Cecil Beaton was given pride of place in her sister Elizabeth's album.[18]

The Princess wore her twenty-first birthday dress once more in Paris: on 21 November 1951 she attended the Franco-British ball held at the Centre Interallié to raise funds for the British Hospital. It was the high point of her visit to the capital. Her appearance in a Dior gown was met with enthusiasm by Parisian onlookers, who had spent hours waiting for her arrival in the pouring rain, thrilled by the thought of seeing a real princess. The next day, after lunch at the Elysée Palace with President Vincent Auriol, she paid another visit to the House of Dior, discovering the Colifichets boutique in the company of the couturier before attending the presentation of the Autumn–Winter 1951 collection in the grand salon. During the show, she took a cigarette from a gold case and held it in a long black cigarette holder.

'I would like to know what has become of the models I saw here two years ago,' she said to Christian Dior, even remembering their first names.[19] Margaret's affability made her highly popular: the French papers nicknamed her '*la Petite*' or '*l'Exquise*'.

L'Exquise and Christian Dior met for the last time on 3 November 1954, at Blenheim Palace, the home of the Duke and Duchess of Marlborough in Oxfordshire, for a charity show in aid of the British Red Cross organized by Alexandra Spencer-Churchill, the Duchess of Marlborough herself. Two thousand guests paid 5 guineas each to attend a presentation of the 161 models in the new *H* line. At 6 pm, ballet music started to play and the show began. It lasted two hours: the models paraded through six adjoining rooms in the palace, one of which was the 'long library', a full 310 metres (340 yards) long – quite a considerable distance when one has several turns to make in high heels. The Dior models – among them Victoire, Alla, Lucky, Odile and Paule – put on a marvellous show, smiling every step of the way.

Left **PAOLO ROVERSI** 2007
Pages 210–11 **ANNIE LEIBOVITZ** 2015

GUY BOURDIN 1971

214

The event went down in history and was repeated on 12 November 1958 – again at Blenheim, again in aid of the British Red Cross and again in the presence of Princess Margaret – but this time without Christian Dior. The couturier's unexpected death a year earlier meant that the house of Dior was now in the hands of his second, the young Yves Mathieu-Saint-Laurent.

The complicity that existed between Princess Margaret and Dior offered two complementary portrayals of the New Look. The couturier expressed in fashion what the Princess embodied in the eyes of the world. Dior's dresses heralded a return to splendour, as did Margaret whenever she wore them. Each in their own way answered an avid desire for novelty and change. A touch of dream and glamour was exactly what was needed to forget the dark days of war and believe in a radiant future. The New Look was there to bring just that.

At the British court, the New Look went hand in hand with a return to pomp and ceremony, which culminated in the celebrations for the coronation of Queen Elizabeth II. Christian Dior had paid homage to what would be the main event of 1953 a few months earlier in January, when he included a royal presentation in his Spring–Summer 1953 collection, which featured a number of Edwardian-style necklines. Coiffed in a Florentine cap, young Brigitte, the daughter of the Baronne de Turckheim – whose nickname was 'Tutu' and who managed the models' dressing room – entered the grand salon in a white faille procession dress with a short train, holding aloft a cushion on which a purple velvet crown ringed with an ermine border was laid. She was followed by a regal-looking Marie-Thérèse, dressed in a diadem and the *Clelia* evening gown, which featured a wealth of embroidery by Rébé. The journalists, buyers, clients and friends in attendance were charmed by Brigitte and captivated by Marie-Thérèse. They marvelled at Christian Dior. 'To see a collection of Dior's dresses filing past gives one the pleasure of watching a spectacular and romantic pageant,' commented Cecil Beaton.[20]

Christian Dior was a born romantic. His swirling ball gowns beautifully revived the ideal vision of a 'Watteau-style' beauty infused with melancholy, the kind that befits royal princesses and for which Beaton's portrait of Margaret stood as an allegory. 'He possesses an exquisite sense of chic and fashion, what one might call beauty which passes, and this gift has made him one of the princes of English society,' said Dior of his friend.[21] There was a rival approaching Beaton's turf, however: the other 'prince' whom everyone was starting to talk about, Antony Armstrong-Jones. Beaton knew him well; he was a friend of his mother – *née* Anne Messel, who became the Comtesse de Rosse on her second marriage – and of his uncle, the famous stage designer Oliver Messel, whom he had photographed many times. There was therefore no question of there being a conflict between Antony Armstrong-Jones and his elder, especially since each had their own way of working.

Above **SARAH MOON** 2014
Right **TOM ORDOYNO** 2014

GUY BOURDIN 1959

After a six-month post as an assistant to the society photographer Baron, Antony Armstrong-Jones set off to conquer London, armed with his Leica camera. Influenced by the work of Cartier-Bresson, he shot scenes from real life of royal guardsmen, workmen, bankers and strippers. He also took fashion photographs and found a way into the best society weddings, dinners and balls thanks to his impressive address book. 'He knows everybody', wrote Audrey Withers, editor-in-chief of British *Vogue* at the time, in a letter to her director, whom she wanted to convince to hire this new talent. In October 1956, Armstrong-Jones signed a contract with *Vogue*.[22] One of his first missions was in Callian, in the South of France. In February 1957 the photographer arrived at the Château de La Colle Noire to shoot a portrait of the proprietor, Christian Dior. On receiving the pictures, Audrey Withers was thrilled: 'I must tell you how delighted I am with the photographs you did for us ... I think the Dior set is a real achievement, for although such a charming person he is genuinely shy – and camera shy – and I can imagine that it took all your tact to break this down.'[23] Dior was indeed camera-shy, especially in private. His friend Cecil Beaton had photographed him in his townhouse on Boulevard Jules-Sandeau in Paris a little earlier in 1953, in a rare series of private photos.

Antony Armstrong-Jones, who became the Earl of Snowdon after his marriage to Princess Margaret, continued his prolific career as a reporter, a portrait photographer of royals, aristocrats, society figures and artists, and occasionally as a fashion photographer. In this latter field, one of his most memorable series was published in British *Vogue* in September 1985. It featured Isabelle Pasco in some of the most beautiful haute couture creations of the season, including a violet satin evening ensemble designed by Marc Bohan for Dior. She stood next to a whippet against a backdrop of a topiaried garden, similar to those that Le Nôtre designed for Louis XIV. Isabelle Pasco photographed by Snowdon is reminiscent of Margaret by Beaton: dressed in their Dior gowns, they both seem to have stepped out of a fairy tale, embodying a moment of youth and grace that lasts for eternity.

Portrait art – in the modern sense of the term – first appeared in the canvases of the fifteenth-century Dutch masters and has been taken up as an essential theme by fashion photographers, some of whom choose to stress the pictorial aspect of their shots, in the same vein as pictorialism. Such was the case for Cecil Beaton, as we have seen – though Edward Steichen, who was a pictorialist, criticized him for viewing photography too much in terms of painting – as well as for Lillian Bassman, Sarah Moon, Deborah Turbeville, Paolo Roversi, David Seidner, Javier Vallhonrat or, more recently, Willy Vanderperre.

The Belgian photographer represents an aesthetic approach that is at once classic and novel. With a static pose, formal sobriety, cold mannerism, milky lighting and a serene facial glow, he has captured sensitive and sombre portraits of budding young girls who turn into icons through his camera lens. A graduate of the legendary Antwerp Fine Arts

Academy, Vanderperre was impressed by the Flemish masters such as Robert Campin, Jan van Eyck and Rogier van der Weyden. This is evidently a passion he shares with his friend Raf Simons, whom he met on the terrace of the Witzli Poetzli, a trendy café in the shadow of the Cathedral of Our Lady in Antwerp. 'We share a lot of the same obsessions and references,' Vanderperre said in 2014. 'I started documenting his shows. It was sometimes a video, other times an image or a series – it was all very organic. We have been working together ever since. It's a collaboration I deeply cherish.'[24]

'There's always a powerful sense of nostalgia for youth – like a memory,' Raf Simons has commented about Willy Vanderperre's work. 'It's not something I can really define or analyse; it's something much more intimate that we all feel and share.'[25] Vanderperre had a perfect grasp of Raf Simons' 'modern romanticism' expressed at Dior, where the Belgian designer engaged in an invigorating review of haute couture.[26] 'It is a matter of confronting the past with the future, the radicalism of youth and the established values of haute couture,' Simons explained, developing in each collection a style lexicon that he shares with Christian Dior.[27] Flowers are one of their mutual passions: 'I am obsessed by flowers, as was Christian Dior.'[28]

Simons comes from Neerpelt, a town in the Limburg province in the Flemish region of Belgium: 'My background was very romantic, surrounded by nature.'[29] This enchanting setting echoes the world Christian Dior grew up in as a child, and which he looked back on 'with tenderness as well as amazement'.[30] Perched on a clifftop exposed to the ocean winds, the family property in Granville was not a particularly favourable environment for horticulture. Despite these obstacles, Christian's mother, Madeleine, was a wonderful gardener who tamed the forces of nature and magnified their beauty in her landscaping. The grounds that surrounded the family home were her work, which her son Christian observed with emotion. Flowers held a very special place in Dior's life and his work as a couturier in particular.

The flower is the essential New Look metaphor. With the war over, the time had come for Christian Dior to fill the world with flowers again. 'I designed clothes for flower-like women, with rounded shoulders, full feminine busts, and hand-span waists above enormous spreading skirts'.[31] Dior likened these skirts to flower 'corollas' and *Corolle* was the name he gave to his very first couture line: 'In the autumn, this trend was emphasized still more. The corollas curved outwards'.[32] The New Look and its pretty petals celebrated the return of heightened femininity. It struck like a whirlwind. Filled with red, yellow and white tulips, the salons of the couture house buzzed with excitement when Dior presented the *Tulipe* line in January 1953. The colours were inspired by the Impressionists' paintings and the fields of flowers that Renoir and Van Gogh loved to paint. One year later, the *Muguet* line was inspired by Dior's love for lily-of-the-valley, a flower that the couturier –

BERT STERN 1964

renowned for being superstitious – considered lucky. *Muguet* would also be used as a name for a lingerie gown, an afternoon dress, a sable jacket, an evening gown and a short evening ensemble, featuring an organdie dress studded with lily-of-the-valley bellflowers.[33] Other models with evocative names also bloomed in Dior's collections: *Hortensia, Coquelicot, Marguerite, Iris, Gardénia, Patchouli, Petunia, Dahlia, Lys*, not to mention veritable bouquets of roses: *Rose France, Rose de Damas, Rose d'avril, Rose de Noël, Rose Pompon, Fête des Roses.*

Embroidered, woven, or pinned to a hat, flowers have remained an obvious inspiration for Christian Dior's colleagues and successors, starting with his beloved Mitzah Bricard, who created hats and accessories. 'Her love of the country and nature does not go further than the flowers with which she decorates her hats and her dresses', commented the couturier.[34] Photographed by Guy Bourdin in one of his most legendary pictures, bees and flies settled on the face of the mannequin Rose-Marie, attracted by the lily-of-the-valley and the cherries which Mitzah had sewn on a black straw and tulle broad-brimmed hat (p. 221).[35] Gianfranco Ferré honoured Dior's lucky lily-of-the-valley in his first collection for the couture house, in a bouquet embroidered by Lesage on the bustier of an evening gown.[36] The Italian couturier also adopted a former reference with pink, red and lilac tulips cascading down a ball gown.[37] The large stylized red poppies printed on a party dress designed by Yves Saint Laurent also come to mind.[38] These in turn inspired a silk chiffon dress designed by John Galliano in 2005.[39] Marc Bohan printed daisies onto an evening gown, as symbols of pure and innocent love.[40] A sign of intense yet fleeting happiness, multicoloured anemones adorn an impressive hat photographed by Bert Stern for the cover of US *Vogue*.[41]

The language of flowers has always bloomed in Dior style, particularly with the arrival of Raf Simons. Roses, orchids, mimosa, zinnia, goldenrod, and delphiniums in their thousands featured floor to ceiling in the salons of a very 'couture' mansion in Paris: it was this stunning décor that the new creative director chose for his first Dior collection on 2 July 2012. 'I love nature, I love flowers. That's so simple and so liberating and it's something that can be understood by everybody, everywhere.'[42] The corolla dresses in the collection confirmed the bucolic tribute. As soon as the show was over, Paolo Roversi photographed some of the models, posing with fragile grace in these emblematic silhouettes. Seated in the middle of the picture, Jac Jagaciak evokes the romanticism of Empress Eugénie surrounded by her maids of honour in the painting by Franz Xaver Winterhalter. Published in *Vanity Fair* magazine to celebrate Simons' appointment at the venerable couture house, Roversi's photo-painting of these blooming princesses stands as a symbol: *Femmes-fleurs* will forever be honoured at the heart of the House of Dior.[43]

Right **BRUCE WEBER** 2014
Pages 232–33 **PAOLO ROVERSI** 2012

Muses

One day in 1919, a fortune-teller whispered the following words to Christian Dior: 'Women are lucky for you, and through them you will achieve success.'[1] Dior was fourteen years old and the prediction made such an impression on him that he would remember it all his life long. The future proved the clairvoyant right: Christian Dior was indeed something of a 'ladies' man' – insofar as he became their favourite couturier. Women surrounded him: the women in his entourage, the women he dressed and the women who inspired him. He was always happy to talk about women in general, but proved much more discreet when it came to evoking one woman in particular, who, collection after collection, was always at the forefront of his mind: his mother Madeleine (a name with a Proustian echo), who left her mark on his astonishing New Look.

Our image of Madeleine Dior is shrouded in mystery: romantic and melancholic, she loved to spend time in the enchanting garden of her villa at Granville, overlooking the sea on the Normandy coast. She might have resembled Nicole Kidman in a photograph by Annie Leibovitz. With her porcelain complexion, glossy hair, regal poise and curvaceous figure dressed in a strict jacket and long skirt, the Australian actress conjures up the memory of Marie-Madeleine Juliette Martin, who in 1898 married Maurice Dior, an industrialist who made his fortune in fertilizers and detergents. The couple had five children: Raymond (1900), Christian (1905), Jacqueline (1909), Bernard (1910) and Ginette, nicknamed Catherine (1917). The young Diors were brought up with the rigour that was to be expected of the upper middle classes. Christian nonetheless managed to escape the supervision of his 'Fräulein' (governess) to spend time close to his mother, with whom he shared a passion for flowers. The garden in Granville summed up his mental world.

Maurice Dior's prosperous affairs led the family to move from Granville to Paris in 1909. The capital was the point from which France radiated around the world, and the City of Light mesmerized young Christian: 'I thank heaven I lived in Paris in the last years of the Belle Epoque. They marked me for life. My mind retains the picture of a time full of happiness, exuberance, and peace, in which everything was directed towards the art of living.'[2] It was a blissful time perfumed with acacia and patchouli, when women perfected the art of adornment with feathers, lace, embroideries and frills. 'I was impressed by women's appearance', Dior confided to his friend, Cecil Beaton. 'Like all children, I inevitably looked at an elegant lady with admiration.'[3] When Dior launched his couture house, he remembered the dresses that celebrated the glorious curves of splendidly starched ladies and invented a New Look that was paradoxically driven by childhood nostalgia. Sadly, his mother would never know it.

When his mother died of septicaemia following an operation in 1931, Christian was twenty-six and running an art gallery with his friend Jacques Bonjean. After somewhat listless studies at the Institut des Etudes Politiques in Paris, followed by the inevitable bout of military service, the bohemian young Dior had managed (though not without difficulty) to convince his parents to give him the capital he needed to open an art gallery. There he exhibited and sold works by Picasso, Braque, Matisse and Dufy, along with emerging talents such as his friends Christian Bérard, Salvador Dalí, Max Jacob and the Berman brothers. His mother would not live to know what came next: 'Looking back on it now I see that it was fortunate that her death came when it did, although it marked me for life. My mother left us before she knew of the perilous future unfolding before us.'[4] Madeleine would not have to experience the bankruptcy of her husband, who lost everything in the aftermath of the Wall Street Crash of 1929. But nor would she ever discover the second career of her son, the young Dior with decidedly unconventional ideas.

In 1932, after closing the gallery he ran with Jacques Bonjean, Christian struck up a new gallery partnership with another friend, Pierre Colle. The economic crisis forced it to close within two years. In early 1934, Dior was stricken with tuberculosis and went to convalesce in Font-Romeu, a town in the Pyrenées-Orientales region. It was here at an altitude of 1,800 metres (6,000 feet) that he embarked on a dizzying new destiny. 'The disease and the cure created a break in my life. Before, I worked with paintings through which painters expressed their personality. Afterwards, once I was cured, I too wanted to find my own self-expression and I started to design dresses.'[5]

'I discovered my true métier – at the age of thirty', acknowledged Christian Dior, who until then had never earned a living.[6] Encouraged by his designer friends – Jean Ozenne (a cousin of Christian Bérard) and his companion Max Kenna – the apprentice couturier trained in the art of illustration. He scraped a living through his drawings, which he sold to *Le Figaro* and to couture houses such as Schiaparelli, Maggy Rouff, Jean Patou, Nina Ricci, Molyneux, Balenciaga or Robert Piguet, to name the most well-known among them.

Left **PATRICK DEMARCHELIER** 1997
Above **NATHANIEL GOLDBERG** 1999

IRVING PENN 1997

In June 1938, Dior was hired by Piguet, for whom he designed exclusive models, including *Café anglais*, a dress with a very wide skirt, which was his first notable success and a foretaste of the New Look. The designer's initial success was cut short by the war, when he was mobilized to Mehun-sur-Yèvre in the Cher region for almost a year. After being declared unfit for service, Christian joined his father, sister Catherine and governess Marthe, who were living a simple life in Callian in the Var region in the farthest southeastern corner of France. He farmed their plot of land and resumed work as an illustrator, long-distance. When Piguet offered him a job once again, Dior hesitated before returning to Paris to take it, but the position had been filled. Thanks to his friend Paul Caldaguès from *Le Figaro*, he was introduced to Lucien Lelong, who hired him as a designer in late 1941. Five years later, in 1946, Dior set up his own couture house. In 1947 he triumphed.

The fortune-teller from Granville had been right: 'Women are lucky for you, and through them you will achieve success.'[7] It began with the women who worked with him from the start: Raymonde Zehnacker, Marguerite Carré, Suzanne Luling and Mitzah Bricard. Mitzah was born Germaine Louise Neustadt in the first year of the twentieth century. Her father was Viennese, her mother was English and she came from an apparently wealthy family. Not much more than this is known – a veil of mystery that merely enhances her legend. Her fashion vocation is said to have appeared at an early age, on the race courses where elegant society ladies, be they aristocrats or demi-mondaines, would parade in the most marvellous dresses. The beautiful Mitzah is said to have married an exiled Russian prince when she was seventeen, though nothing actually proves this was true. It is also said that she may have had numerous protectors, all of whom were ready to cover her in jewels. The conditional certainly trumps the indicative in her story.

There was no doubt, however, about Germaine's marriage to the diplomat Alexandre Biano. In 1926, Germaine Biano began her career as a designer at Mirande-Doucet, where she spent four years dressing what remained of Jacques Doucet's prestigious clientele. Doucet had been one of the leading couturiers of the Belle Epoque and Germaine acquired a perfect knowledge of the traditions of couture, as exclusive as it is demanding. 'I hate things that are half-good,' she was known to say. She then joined Edward Molyneux, the Irish couturier located on Rue Royale. Molyneux designed dresses in simple, sober cuts and discreet colours – beige, grey and pastel tones – that pleased an aesthetic clientele with scant inclination for eye-catching novelties. Here Germaine established what would become her inimitable style. Is this the point at which she became Mitzah? No one can remember.

MITZAH BRICARD **CECIL BEATON** c. 1950

HENRY CLARKE 1957

Christian Dior loved Molyneux – 'It is certainly Molyneux's style that has most influenced me'[8] – and was smitten by Mitzah, a woman for whom elegance was the 'sole raison d'être.'[9] It was 1940 and with Europe at war, the Irish couturier returned to London and the ambassadress of chic joined Balenciaga to create hats. In 1941 after the death of her husband, Germaine married Hubert Bricard, the Managing Director of BLB Laboratories, and she officially retired from fashion until Christian Dior contacted her in 1946. Mitzah was forty-six and still full of panache. 'Gazing at life out of the windows of the Ritz,' was how her bashful friend Christian put it.[10] 'Luxury is the only necessity', acknowledged Mitzah from behind her hat veil – the vital accessory for blurring the blandness of reality. 'She had an infallible intuition about what a woman should wear in order to seduce,' recalled Marc Bohan, who worked with her later. 'She was frivolity itself, sometimes a little eccentric, a spirit of extravagance in luxury.' Every day for twenty years, this guru of good taste set sparks flying at 30 Avenue Montaigne.

The House of Dior was accustomed to feverish periods of activity; the hushed salons drew journalists, buyers, friends, famous clients and worldwide stars. 'No international star today can dress anywhere other than Paris without losing their prestige,' stated *Elle* magazine.[11] In May 1947, Rita Hayworth checked into the George V hotel with eight trunks and forty suitcases. The Columbia movie star was on a visit to the French capital before going to Cannes, travelling back via Paris and then to England to promote her new film, *Gilda*. She was informed about the New Look and promptly ordered a dozen models from Christian Dior, all identical to the dresses worn by his mannequins, along with several replicas of their high-heeled shoes. She wore *Soirée* (a long organza gown from the *Corolle* line) to the première of *Gilda* in Paris. Back in New York, the American beauty posed for Horst P. Horst in one of her new Dior dresses, *Maxim's*, with its large bows at the *décolleté*: a very chiaroscuro glamour.

Horst was famous for his portraits of stars, most of which were shot during the 1930s and 1940s. He opened his magnificent portfolio with the English actress Gertrude Lawrence in 1931. Two images were published in British and US *Vogue* to stunning effect, leading Condé Nast to open up the doors to the *Vogue* studios in New York. It was there that he photographed Bette Davis, Olivia de Havilland, Ginger Rogers, Joan Crawford, Gene Tierney, Paulette Goddard, Loretta Young and Marlene Dietrich – the latter on two occasions, once before and once after the New Look. In 1942 Dietrich wore the fashion of wartime, as seen in her broad-shouldered black alpaca suit and what Horst called her 'terrible hat' (in those days the stars posed in their own clothes and the photographer had to put up with it).[12]

Above **CAMILLA AKRANS** 2007
Right RITA HAYWORTH **HORST P. HORST** 1947

Above and left **PAOLO ROVERSI** 2005

Five years later the Paramount star returned with her daughter Maria and her 'new look': she had attended Christian Dior's second presentation in August 1947 and ordered no fewer than ten models, including an adaptation of *Chandernagor*, with its 'spirited line'.[13] This was the dress she wore for Horst, first in a shot with her daughter, also dressed in Dior (the shot that US *Vogue* published), then alone, standing proud and solemn.[14]

In the years after World War II, American movie stars were the stuff of dreams for Europe, particularly in France. Imposed in 1939 and maintained even after the Liberation, the law banning American films was repealed by the Blum-Byrnes agreement in 1947. After fierce negotiations, the United States cleared part of France's debt in return for exorbitant privileges, including abolishing the quota of American films. This opened the way for Hollywood movies, much to the ire of the French Communist party and film industry unions. American celebrities travelled to Paris, where they inevitably fell for the sophisticated fashion of Christian Dior, whose reputation had reached all the way to California.

In 1947, spectators (420 million of them) flocked to the cinema to discover the Hollywood super-productions that turned their heroines into goddesses blessed with flawless beauty. The stars – Rita Hayworth, Ava Gardner, Grace Kelly and Lauren Bacall – dressed in Dior, 'on screen and on the town',[15] and became the muses of the famous couture house thanks to their style and their image. In the 2005 Autumn–Winter haute couture collection, John Galliano dedicated seven flamboyant dresses to them, named *Rita, Marlène, Ava, Ginger, Olivia, Vivien* and *Lauren*.

When Lauren Bacall and Humphrey Bogart passed through Paris on their way to Africa in 1951 – where 'Bogey' was due to film John Huston's *The African Queen* – they attended the presentation of the Dior collection at Avenue Montaigne. Bacall did not order any dresses – 'I will think about it', she told *Elle* – but succumbed later, choosing a chiffon dancing dress with a brown butterfly print (*Pantomime*). She wore it in public for the Academy Awards ceremony a year later, on 20 March 1952, when her husband was awarded the Oscar for Best Actor in *African Queen*. 'Dior's dresses were dramatic and made an impression,' Bacall recounted. 'And suddenly to be able to say, "I have a Dior and how about that" – it spoke volumes'.[16] Elizabeth Taylor, Reese Witherspoon and Jennifer Lawrence each wore Dior to receive their Oscar for Best Actress in 1961 (*Butterfield 8*), 2006 (*Walk the Line*) and 2013 (*Happiness Therapy*) respectively.

They may not all walk away with a golden statuette, but global film stars do leave a dazzling trace on the red carpet, asserting their influence on fashion.

Above **DOMINIQUE ISSERMANN** 1994
Right **MAX VADUKUL** 1992
Pages 258–59 **LUCIANA VAL** & **FRANCO MUSSO** 2008

MARILYN MONROE **BERT STERN** 1962

In magazines today, models at the top of their profession have to make room for 'star models' posing for fashion spreads – a vogue that Marilyn Monroe heralded back in 1962, when she was photographed by Bert Stern.

Stern was at the pinnacle of his art when he convinced Marilyn to sit for him and have the pictures published in *Vogue*; it was the first time the US edition featured a portrait of the star. 'I'd bought a whole bunch of clothes for her to choose from,' recalled Babs Simpson, the fashion editor dispatched to cover the shoot at the Bel-Air hotel. 'I tried to guide her into what looked best.'[17] Stern produced a breathtaking image of the famous sex symbol, dressed in black by Dior.[18] It was to become known as the actress's legendary 'Last Sitting': six weeks later Marilyn died, just as *Vogue* was going to print.

Right CHARLIZE THERON **PATRICK DEMARCHELIER** 2012
Pages 264–65 NATALIE PORTMAN **PAOLO ROVERSI** 2014

Dior's Guidelines

1947–1957. Ten years, twenty-two collections, twenty-four lines and a rapid succession of 'new looks'.[1] Christian Dior's oeuvre lasted only a decade, but it was prolific and an example in fashion. 'Nobody has ever constructed a language as rich and clear as Dior's in such a short space of time,' says Raf Simons.[2] That Dior revolutionized fashion by giving women their femininity back is a statement that never dies. Born from a simple idea, the New Look that he devised in 1947 would be the stroke of genius that brought him the ultimate glory. 'Thinking about it today, I love the idea that someone can kick the pedestal out from the establishment,' says Raf Simons.[3] Dior's instant success could have paralysed him and eliminated any potential future, but the 'young' couturier, who was forty-two when he finally launched his dream, had all the makings of a prodigy.

In his farewell address to his friend, Jean Cocteau evoked 'the charming genius with which he transcended the frivolous imperative of fashion'.[4] It is true that Dior was a master in the art of making fashion exciting, offering it the luxury of total transformation from one collection to the next. 'He brought in the idea that each season had to bring a change to the new line, whereas beforehand fashion evolved much more slowly ... he aroused curiosity and expectation among the audience, for whom the couturier became a kind of magician.'[5]

Christian Dior blithely launched a host of stunning ideas – the Dior 'bombs' that the press, buyers and clients awaited with avid curiosity. 'We waited for the scandal, the "He's exaggerating ... It's a disguise ... Sheer folly ..." But he didn't exaggerate, it wasn't a disguise and there were no follies – or very few, at least ... And that was the best way to be sensational,' wrote Françoise Giroud after the presentation of the Spring–Summer 1948 collection.[6]

After the *Corolle* and *En 8* lines launched the hysteria of the New Look, Christian Dior gave dresses the edgy movement and style of a sketch – the *Zig-Zag* line – or dreamed up an ample line taking flight in the *Envol* line. In winter 1948, a dropped shoulder was accentuated by a brand-new cut for sleeves that looked like wings – the *Ailée* line. Christian Dior was a skilled cutter, an 'architect of the trade', commented Gianfranco Ferré, a trained architect himself who would go on to produce for the House of Dior the same kinds of graphic effects around a fabulous collar or pockets with oversized flaps.[7]

'I wanted to be an architect: as a couturier, I am obliged to follow architectural rules and principles,' Christian Dior confessed.[8] Though his parents thwarted his vocation, Dior ended up returning to his first love from an unexpected angle: haute couture. 'I think of my work as ephemeral architecture, dedicated to the beauty of the female body,' he proclaimed.[9] 'When you see Dior's silhouettes, they always appear very delicate and feminine,' Raf Simons explains. 'But if you analyse the shapes and delve into the cuts, you see that they are often extremely complex, incredibly innovative and highly architectured. However architectured its cut may be, he wanted a piece of clothing to be loved, understood and perceived as attractive by lots of women.'[10]

Which piece will open the show? Raf Simons would have obviously asked himself this question as the presentation of his first haute couture collection drew near (Autumn–Winter 2012). Christian Dior's fifth successor chose 'the *Bar* jacket, so characteristic of the New Look.'[11] Now the twirling skirt was gone: today's woman wears trousers, her hands thrust in the pockets. The *Bar* had become a dinner suit as well as a coat or a dress, but had kept the same architectural principle: 'it's more the engineering that has evolved,' the former industrial designer noted.[12]

When he discovered the house archives, Raf Simons carefully examined the collections from 1947 to 1957. 'Everything is there in the first ten years. All the codes, the waist, the bust, the hips, the belts and numerous other small details . . . All these codes that I still find so beautiful and modern.'[13] Simons remixed – to use a contemporary term – the lines that Dior left as his legacy. For his first ready-to-wear collection (Spring–Summer 2013), he revisited the *Bar* jacket and the 'corolla' skirts sprinkled with roses; he also took inspiration from the *Ailée* line (Autumn–Winter 1948) and one of its highlights: *Coquette*, a gala ball gown in pearl-grey satin, whose décolleté used a lapping technique, to come up with an extra-mini version in duchesse satin covered in organza, to be worn over black wool shorts. A bustier-tuxedo dress recalled *Camaïeu*, a bustier-sheath dress with a satin yoke at the front that suggested tuxedo lapels (*Milieu du siècle* line, Autumn–Winter 1949 collection). There were also several A-line dresses, evoking the eponymous line for Spring–Summer 1955. In Dior chronology, the *A* line fits between the *H* and the *Y*: after gambling on length and a slimline bust (*H* line, Autumn–Winter 1954) and before going for a tighter, higher waist that lengthened legs to the maximum (*Y* line, Autumn–Winter 1955), Dior imagined a free-flowing flared line with slim shoulders and a wide skirt, resembling a capital A. A look at even just a few of these lines shows that Dior in no way positioned himself as the guardian of an unchanging style, but as a creator of ephemeral trends full of inventiveness and surprise, the looks women dream of all over the world.

Right CATE BLANCHETT **WILLY VANDERPERRE** 2013
Pages 270–71 MARION COTILLARD **JEAN-BAPTISTE MONDINO** 2012

From 1947 to 1957: Dior had just ten years to achieve his meteoric rise, during which he surpassed himself over and over again, amazing everyone who had been fooled by his modesty and restraint. Contrary to all expectations, he restored the prestige of haute couture at a time when it seemed under the greatest threat, turning himself into one of the most dazzling symbols of couture's golden age – *'l'âge Dior'*. 'He represented better than any other his time: the postwar period when everything seemed easy, when luxury was not insolent and when beauty opened every door,' Yves Saint Laurent recalled. 'Still, each time I reread magazines from the 1950s, Christian Dior's magisterial talent astonishes me.'[14] Page after page, in images shot by the greatest photographers, the full force of Dior's creations stands out. Contemplated in all their diversity, they allow the Dior name to flourish supreme, a synthesis of excellence and elegance *à la française* in the eyes of the world. The couture house at 30 Avenue Montaigne brilliantly upholds its founder's favourite motto: *Je maintiendrai.* Christian Dior has gone, but Dior remains.

MERT ALAS & **MARCUS PIGGOTT** 2007

Left **FRANCES MCLAUGHLIN** 1952
Pages 284–85 **NICK KNIGHT** 2008

283

MUCH
WAS
DECIDED
BEFORE
YOU WERE
BORN

YOU
MUST
HAVE
ONE
GRAND
PASSION

MODERATION
KILLS
THE
SPIRIT

PRIVATE PROPERTY CREATED CRIME
EXPRESSING
IS
REDISTRIBUTING WEALTH IS IMPERATIVE

NOTES

PRELUDE (pp. 8–25)

1. Christian Dior, *Dior by Dior*, trans. Antonia Fraser, London: V&A Publishing, 2012 (first published by Weidenfeld & Nicolson, 1957), p. 39.
2. Bettina Graziani, *Bettina par Bettina*, Flammarion, Paris, 1964, pp. 63–64.
3. Bettina Ballard, *In My Fashion*, David McKay Company Inc., New York, 1960, p. 221.
4. *Dior by Dior*, p. 192. The second and third sentences are absent from the English edition.
5. Ibid., p. 32.
6. Irving Penn, *Passage*, Alfred A. Knopf in association with Calloway, New York, 1991, p. 80.
7. *Vanity Fair* US, June 1991, p. 150.
8. *Harper's Bazaar, 100 Years of the American Female*, Random House, New York, 1967, p. 94.
9. Penelope Rowlands, *A Dash of Daring: Carmel Snow and Her Life in Fashion, Art, and Letters*, Atria Books, 2005, p. 334.
10. Norman Parkinson, *Lifework*, Weidenfeld & Nicolson, London, 1983, p. 65.
11. Erwin Blumenfeld, *Studio Blumenfeld: Color, New York, 1941–1960*, Göttingen: Steidl, 2012, p. 198.
12. *Vogue* Paris, September 1961, p. 188; *Harper's Bazaar*, September 1961, p. 211.

CHAPTER 1: FIELD OF DREAMS (pp. 26–67)

1. *M Le Monde*, 14 July 2012, p. 55.
2. *Vogue* Paris, August 1989, p. 182.
3. Christian Dior, *Dior by Dior*, trans. Antonia Fraser, London: V&A Publishing, 2012 (first published by Weidenfeld & Nicolson, 1957).
4. Ibid., p. 79; p. 62.
5. *Combat*, 11 February 1947.
6. *Elle*, 23 April 1990, p. 18.
7. *Dior by Dior*, p. 20.
8. Ibid.
9. Ibid., p. 21.
10. *Petits Poèmes en Prose, Les Paradis Artificiels*, Charles Baudelaire, Librairie Alphonse Lemerre, 1949.
11. *Harper's Bazaar*, May 1947, p. 130.
12. Bettina Ballard, *In My Fashion*, David McKay Company Inc., New York, 1960, p. 237.
13. Denise Dubois-Jallais, *La Tzarine, Hélène Lazareff et l'aventure de 'Elle'*, Robert Laffont, Paris, 1984, pp. 124–125.
14. *Elle*, 28 January 1947, p. 5.
15. *Dior by Dior*, p. 22.
16. Interview with Stanley Garfinkel, 22 January 1984, recording conserved by Dior Héritage.
17. *Dior by Dior*, p. 26.
18. '*Elle* est contente d'*Elle*' ('*Elle* is pleased with *Elle*') was the caption for the outfit that graced the cover of *Elle* on 18 March 1947.
19. Press kit for the Christian Dior Spring–Summer 1947 collection.
20. Françoise Giroud, *Dior*, Éditions du Regard, Paris, 1987, p. 9.
21. *Dior by Dior*, p. 26.
22. Diary of Suzanne Luling, who was the salon director at the House of Christian Dior. This is an unpublished document which Suzanne's cousin, Brigitte Tortet, kindly allowed me to consult.
23. René Clair had just finished filming *Le Silence est d'or*, for which Christian Dior had designed the costumes shortly before starting his first collection. The film was released in France on 21 May 1947.
24. The world of haute couture was not spared by the strikes. The ateliers of the major houses stopped work at collection time, in February 1947. Pressured by the seamstresses of the neighbouring couture houses, Christian Dior had to ask his workers to leave their workstations four days before his first show.

Nearly all of them stayed to finish the collection with friends of the couturier, such as Henri Sauguet, Jean Ozenne, René Gruau and Suzanne Luling, helping out in the ateliers.
25. British *Vogue*, October 1947, p. 35.
26. Extract from speech by George C. Marshall, 5 June 1947, *Foreign Affairs*, May–June 1997, p. 161.
27. *Elle*, 14 September 1948, p. 8.
28. Translator's note: this was translated as 'An Innocent Abroad in the USA' in the English publication of *Dior by Dior*, 1957.
29. *Dior by Dior*, p. 47.
30. Ibid., pp. 47–48.
31. Ibid., p. 22.
32. *Vogue* US, 1 November 1945, p. 160.
33. *Dior by Dior*, p. 5.
34. Ibid., p. 7.
35. Ibid., p. 8.
36. The 5,000 shares of Société Christian Dior capital were each worth 1,000 French francs and were split between various companies in the Boussac group: Société Gaston couturier, 2,706 shares; CIC, 1,000 shares; Filatures Thaon, 450 shares; Filatures et tissages Nomexy, 450 shares; the former Établissements Ziegler, 394 shares. Traditionally, couture houses belonged to the founding couturiers and their descendants. The Société Christian Dior mapped out the future: a house belonging to a large financial group.
37. Marie-France Pochna, *Bonjour, Monsieur Boussac*, Robert Laffont, Paris, 1980, p. 149.
38. *Dior by Dior*, p. 23.
39. Ibid., p. 24.
40. Interview with the author, 11 June 2012.
41. *Women's Wear Daily*, 17 November 1946.
42. Bettina Ballard, *In My Fashion*, David McKay Company, Inc., New York, 1960, p. 236.
43. Along with Winston Churchill, Maurice Chevalier and Rita Hayworth, Christian Dior was one of the four people who 'had the most column inches devoted to them, taking over newspaper front pages the most often,' wrote *Elle* magazine, 8 July 1947, pp. 4–5.
44. *Vogue* Paris, March 1987, p. 292.
45. Press kit for the Christian Dior Autumn–Winter 1947 collection.
46. The 20 January 1948 issue of *Elle* magazine reported that the *Margrave* dress, bought from Dior for 55,000 francs by a few foreign clients, Doris Duke included, was then interpreted in less expensive versions by the major American garment makers, such as Rose Barrack, Macy's, Parnis Livingston, Junior League Frocks and David Westheim.
47. *Elle*, 1 June 1948, p. 3; *Elle*, 15 June 1948, p. 20; *Elle*, 29 June 1948, p. 4.
48. Under the Marshall Plan, exporting a French product to the US gave France dollar credits which it could in turn use to import a product or raw material from the US. The House of Dior therefore made a considerable contribution to relaunching the French economy following World War II.
49. *Paris Match*, 18 March 1950, p. 19.
50. Molière, *The Pretentious Young Ladies*, Act I, Sc. IX, trans. Henri Van Laun, R. Worthington, New York, 1880.
51. *Dior by Dior*, p. 193.

CHAPTER 2: STRIKE A POSE (pp. 68–111)

1. *Harper's Bazaar*, September 1954, p. 197.
2. 'Once again, the backbone of fashion is provided by Balenciaga and Dior and, to a lesser degree, Givenchy', wrote Carmel Snow in the September 1955 issue of *Harper's Bazaar*, p. 205.
3. 'Richard Avedon: Darkness and Light', *American

Masters* season 10, episode 3, 1996.
4. *Harper's Bazaar*, July 1940, p. 56; *Harper's Bazaar*, May 1947, p. 149.
5. 'Richard Avedon: Darkness and Light', *American Masters*.
6. *Smithsonian*, October 2005, p. 22.
7. Michael Gross, *Top Model, les secrets d'un sale business*, A Contrario, Paris, p. 129.
8. *Soirée romaine* dress, Autumn–Winter 1955 collection.
9. *Vanity Fair* US, June 1991, p. 167.
10. Michael Gross, *Top Model, les secrets d'un sale business*, A Contrario, Paris, p. 129.
11. *Soirée de Paris* dress, Autumn–Winter 1955 collection. The sketch of this model is dated July 5, 1955; it was the very first model by Yves Mathieu-Saint-Laurent, who joined Dior on June 20, 1955 as a studio assistant.
12. 'Richard Avedon: Darkness and Light', *American Masters*. It is noteworthy that *Dovima with Elephants* does not feature among the 284 photos compiled in *An Autobiography*, Avedon's memoirs published by Random House in 1993.
13. Richard Avedon and Truman Capote, *Observations*, New York: Simon & Schuster, 1959, p. 26.
14. Dovima's pseudonym comes from the first letters of her three Christian names: Dorothy Virginia Margaret.
15. *The Fashion Insider*, 12 February 2014.
16. 'Mode 6' TV show broadcast on M6, 13 March 1994.
17. *Dépêche Mode*, February 1995, p. 42.
18. *Vogue* Paris, May 2005, p. 221.
19. Diana Vreeland, *Allure*, Garden City New York, Doubleday & Co. Inc., 1980, p. 164.
20. *V*, Spring 2013, p. 160.
21. *Dior by Dior*, p. 59.

CHAPTER 3: THE RETURN OF ROMANCE (pp. 112–85)

1. *Dior by Dior*, p. 36.
2. Ibid., p. 21.
3. *Vogue* Paris, November 1951, p. 82.
4. *Vogue* US, 15 August 1947, p. 157.
5. *Dior by Dior*, p. 36.
6. *Vogue* US, 15 August 1948, p. 158.
7. *Dior by Dior*, p. 36.
8. 300,000 francs, according to *Elle* dated 1 October 1948, p. 3.
9. Christian Dior, *The Little Dictionary of Fashion*, V&A Publications, London, 2007, p. 13.
10. Natasha Fraser-Cavassoni, *Once Upon A Time Monsieur Dior*, The Pointed Leaf Press, New York, p. 103.
11. Interview with the author, 11 June 2012.
12. Carole Weisweiller, *Jean Marais, le bien-aimé*, Patrick Renaudot, Rocher, 2002, p. 354.
13. Penelope Rowlands, *A Dash of Daring: Carmel Snow and Her Life in Fashion, Art, and Letters*, Atria Books, 2005, p. 162.
14. Deborah Mitford, Duchess of Devonshire, *Wait For Me!*, John Murray, London, 2010, p. 286.
15. One of the giant costumes, which stands 270 cm tall, is today conserved at the Dalí theatre-museum in Figueres, Spain.
16. *Harper's Bazaar*, December 1997, p. 194.
17. *Dior by Dior*, p. 36.
18. Ibid., p. 168.
19. Excerpt from Suzanne Luling's diary. See note 22, chapter 1.
20. *Dior by Dior*, pp. 178–179.
21. Ibid., p. 34.
22. Ibid., p. 171.
23. Yves Saint Laurent, *Bravo Yves*, 1982, p. 31.
24. Spring–Summer 1948 collection.
25. Autumn–Winter 1957 collection.

26. Autumn–Winter 1957 collection.
27. Spring–Summer 1949, Autumn–Winter 1952, Spring–Summer 1955, Autumn–Winter 1956 collections.
28. Spring–Summer 1955 collection.
29. Spring–Summer 1949, Autumn–Winter 1952, Autumn–Winter 1953, Spring–Summer 1955, Spring–Summer 1956, Spring–Summer 1957, Autumn–Winter 1957 collections.
30. Spring–Summer 1955, Spring–Summer 1956 collections.
31. Spring–Summer 1956 collection.
32. Spring–Summer 1956 collection.
33. Spring–Summer 1956 collection.
34. Autumn–Winter 1957 collection.
35. Autumn–Winter 1953, Autumn–Winter 1954, Spring–Summer 1956, Autumn–Winter 1957 collections.
36. Christian Dior, *Christian Dior & moi*, bibliothèque Amiot-Dumont, Paris, 1956, p. 235 (not in the English edition).
37. Press kit for the Spring–Summer 1955 collection (*A* line).
38. Press kit for the Spring–Summer 1952 collection (*Sinueuse* line).
39. *Dior by Dior*, p. 34.
40. Colombe Pringle, *Roger Vivier*, collection Mémoire de la Mode, Assouline, Paris, 1998, p. 8.
41. *Vogue* Paris, September 1983, p. 367.
42. *Vogue* Paris, March 1996, p. 158.
43. Ibid., p. 7.
44. *Knack*, 14 December 2012, p. 24.
45. Press kit, Autumn–Winter 2014 haute couture collection.
46. *Madame Figaro*, 23 November 2012, pp. 158–160.
47. Ibid., p. 156.
48. Press kit, Autumn–Winter 2014 haute couture collection.

CHAPTER 4: PRINCESSES IN BLOOM (pp. 186–233)
1. Cecil Beaton, *The Royal Portraits*, Thames & Hudson, London, 1988, p. 148.
2. *Vogue* US, 15 October 1935, p. 61.
3. *Les Hasards heureux de l'escarpolette*, Jean-Honoré Fragonard, 1767–1769.
4. *Elle*, 10 July 1950, p. 19.
5. *Elle*, August 1950, p. 8.
6. Souvenirs de Marion Crawford, *Elle*, 15 May 1950, p. 17.
7. *Le Petit Parc*, Jean-Honoré Fragonard, c. 1762 1763; *Portrait of Molly and Peggy*, Thomas Gainsborough, c. 1760
8. Cecil Beaton, *The Glass of Fashion*, Rizzoli Ex Libris, New York 2014 (reissue), p. 299.
9. *Elle*, 6 April 1948, p. 5.
10. It is interesting to note that the House of Norman Hartnell hired Marc Bohan after he left Dior in 1989. He became the creative director of the famous English couture house from 1990 to 1992.
11. For her wedding on 8 October 1993 to David Armstrong-Jones, Viscount Linley, the son of Princess Margaret and Antony Armstrong-Jones, Serena Stanhope asked the couturier Bruce Robbins to draw inspiration from the *Fidélité* wedding gown created by Christian Dior (for the crinoline) and from Margaret's wedding dress designed by Norman Hartnell (for the bodice). Coincidentally or not, she held a bunch of lily-of-the-valley in her hands, Christian Dior's lucky flower.
12. *The Australian Women's Weekly*, 4 February 1950.
13. Ibid.
14. *The Sunday Times Magazine*, 5 October 1986, p. 56.
15. *Le Figaro*, 25 April 1950, p. 2.

16. *Elle*, 15 May 1950, p. 9.
17. Josephine Ross, *Beaton in Vogue*, Thames & Hudson, London, 2012.
18. *Paris Match*, 23 November 1963, cover.
19. *Elle*, 5 January 1953, p. 21.
20. *The Glass of Fashion*, p. 214.
21. Preface to the French edition of *The Glass of Fashion*, quoted in the 2014 reissue in English, p. 12.
22. Antony Armstrong-Jones, *Snowdon – A Life in View*, Rizzoli, New York, 2014, p. 76.
23. Letter from Audrey Withers to Antony Armstrong-Jones dated February 22, 1957, reproduced in *Snowdon – A Life in View*, p. 109.
24. *Dazed & Confused*, April 2014.
25. *System*, Spring–Summer 2014, p. 71.
26. *Le Figaro*, 11 April 2012.
27. *Knack*, 14 December 2012, p. 24.
28. *Elle*, 13 July 2012, p. 12.
29. *AnOther Magazine*, Spring–Summer 2013, p. 320.
30. *Dior by Dior*, p. 167.
31. Ibid., pp. 22–23.
32. Ibid., p. 143.
33. Spring–Summer 1950 haute couture collection; Autumn–Winter 1950 haute couture collection; Autumn–Winter 1950 haute couture collection; Spring–Summer 1954 haute couture collection; Spring–Summer 1957 haute couture collection.
34. *Dior by Dior*, p. 13.
35. *Vogue* Paris, April 1954, pp. 116–117.
36. The *Duchesse* model, Autumn–Winter 1989 Haute Couture collection entitled *Ascot-Cecil Beaton*.
37. *Eden* model, Spring–Summer 1992 Haute Couture collection.
38. *Nuit de Grenade* model, Spring–Summer 1960 Haute Couture collection.
39. Autumn–Winter 2005 ready-to-wear collection.
40. Spring–Summer 1962 Haute Couture collection.
41. Christian Dior–New York collection, *Vogue* US, 1 February 1964, cover.
42. *AnOther Magazine*, Spring–Summer 2013, p. 321.
43. *Vanity Fair* US, September 2012, pp. 338–339.

CHAPTER 5: MUSES (pp. 234–65)
1. *Dior by Dior*, p. 3.
2. Ibid., p. 171.
3. *The Glass of Fashion*, p. 299.
4. *Dior by Dior*, p. 179.
5. *Elle*, 14 September 1948, p. 9.
6. *Dior by Dior*, p. 184.
7. Ibid.
8. *The Glass of Fashion*, pp. 300–301.
9. *Dior by Dior*, p. 12.
10. Ibid.
11. *Elle*, 1 October 1948, p. 3.
12. Valentine Lawford, *Horst: His Work and His World*, Alfred A. Knopf, New York, 1984, p. 236.
13. 1947 Press kit for the Autumn–Winter collection (*Corolle* line).
14. *Vogue* US, 1 January 1948, p. 144.
15. *Stars en Dior, de l'écran à la ville* (Stars in Dior, From Screen to Streets) is the title of an exhibition that was presented at the Musée Christian Dior in Granville in 2012, revealing the friendly and professional ties that have always existed between the House of Dior and movie stars.
16. *Monsieur Dior. Once Upon a Time*, Natasha Fraser-Cavassoni, The Pointed Leaf Press, New York, 2014, p. 33.
17. Portrait of Babs Simpson (née Beatrice Crosby de Menocal) by Dodie Kazanjian in *Vogue: The Editor's Eye*, Abrams, New York, 2012, p. 22.
18. *Vogue* US, 1 September 1962, pp. 190–191.

CHAPTER 6: DIOR'S GUIDELINES (pp. 266–91)
1. In chronological order: *Corolle* and *En 8*, then *Corolle*, *Zig-Zag* and *Envol*, *Ailée*, *Trompe-l'œil*, *Milieu du siècle*, *Verticale*, *Oblique*, *Naturelle*, *Longue*, *Sinueuse*, *Profilée*, *Tulipe*, *Vivante*, *Muguet*, *H*, *A*, *Y*, *Flèche*, *Aimant*, *Libre* and lastly *Fuseau*.
2. *Les Echos Série limitée*, 14 September 2012.
3. *032c*, Winter 2014, p. 76.
4. *Arts*, 3 October 1957.
5. *Hommage à Christian Dior, 1947–1957*, Union des arts décoratifs, Paris, 1986, p. 17.
6. *Elle*, 24 February 1948, p. 4.
7. *Marie Claire*, September 1989, p. 151.
8. *Conférences écrites par Christian Dior pour la Sorbonne, 1955–1957* [Lectures written by Christian Dior for the Sorbonne], Institut français de la mode – Editions du Regard, Paris, 1997, p. 43.
9. *Dior by Dior*, p. 189.
10. *Vogue* Germany, October 2013, p. 271.
11. *Les Echos Série limitée*, 14 September 2012.
12. Ibid.
13. Ibid.
14. *WWD*, 27 February 2007, section II, p. 10.

CREDITS

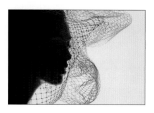

PAGES 2–3
COLLECTION Christian Dior ready-to-wear by John Galliano, autumn/winter 2004
PHOTOGRAPHER Sølve Sundsbø
MODEL Karen Elson
FASHION EDITOR Jonathan Kaye
MAGAZINE *Numéro*, Nov. 2004 (pp. 122–23)
© Sølve Sundsbø/Art + Commerce

PAGE 8
Christian Dior 1947
PHOTOGRAPHER Irving Penn
MAGAZINE *Vogue* USA, Mar. 1987 (p. 479)
Copyright © The Irving Penn Foundation

PAGE 4
COLLECTION Christian Dior ready-to-wear by Raf Simons, spring/summer 2013
PHOTOGRAPHER Willy Vanderperre
MODEL Jennifer Lawrence
FASHION EDITOR Olivier Rizzo
© Willy Vanderperre

PAGE 11
COLLECTION Christian Dior haute couture, spring/summer 1947 (*Bar* suit, *Corolle* line)
PHOTOGRAPHER Jean-Baptiste Mondino
MODEL Marion Cotillard
FASHION EDITOR Friquette Thévenet
MAGAZINE *Dior Magazine*, autumn 2012 (cover)
© Jean-Baptiste Mondino

PAGES 6–7
COLLECTION Christian Dior haute couture by Raf Simons, autumn/winter 2012
PHOTOGRAPHER Mario Testino
MODEL Kate Moss
FASHION EDITOR Sarajane Hoare
MAGAZINE *Vogue* Spain, Dec. 2012 (pp. 268–69)
© Mario Testino

PAGE 12
COLLECTION Christian Dior haute couture, autumn/winter 1950 (*Illusionniste* coat, *Oblique* line)
PHOTOGRAPHER Irving Penn
MODEL Lisa Fonssagrives
FASHION EDITOR Bettina Ballard
MAGAZINE *Vogue* USA, 1 Sept. 1950 (p. 138)
Irving Penn/*Vogue*; © Condé Nast

PAGES 14–15
COLLECTION Christian Dior haute couture,
autumn/winter 1950 (*Embuscade* suit,
Oblique line)
PHOTOGRAPHER Richard Avedon
MODEL Dovima
MAGAZINE *Harper's Bazaar*, Sept. 1950
(pp. 196–97)
© The Richard Avedon Foundation

PAGE 16
COLLECTION Christian Dior haute couture
by Raf Simons, autumn/winter 2012
PHOTOGRAPHER Willy Vanderperre
MODEL Suvi Koponen
FASHION EDITOR Olivier Rizzo
MAGAZINE *Dior Magazine*, autumn 2012
(p. 47)
© Willy Vanderperre

PAGE 17
COLLECTION Christian Dior haute couture
by Marc Bohan, spring/summer 1978
PHOTOGRAPHER Horst P. Horst
MODEL Mounia Orosemane
MAGAZINE *Vogue* Paris, Mar. 1978 (p. 230)
© Horst P. Horst/*Vogue* Paris

PAGE 18
COLLECTION Christian Dior ready-to-wear
by John Galliano, autumn/winter 2005
PHOTOGRAPHER Mario Sorrenti
MODEL Kate Moss
FASHION EDITOR Camilla Nickerson
MAGAZINE *W*, Nov. 2005 (p. 306)
© Mario Sorrenti

PAGE 21
COLLECTION Christian Dior ready-to-wear
by Raf Simons, autumn/winter 2013
PHOTOGRAPHER Patrick Demarchelier
MODEL Sasha Pivovarova
FASHION EDITOR George Cortina
MAGAZINE *Vogue* Japan, Aug. 2013 (cover)
© Patrick Demarchelier – Condé Nast Japan/
Trunk Archive

PAGES 22–23
COLLECTION Christian Dior haute couture
by Raf Simons, spring/summer 2014
PHOTOGRAPHER Tim Walker
MODELS Ola and Mac Rudnicka, unidentified
model, Jake Love, Natalie Westling and
Esmeralda Seay-Reynolds
FASHION EDITOR Edward Enninful
MAGAZINE *W*, Apr. 2014 (pp. 106–7)
© Tim Walker

PAGES 24–25
COLLECTION Christian Dior haute couture
by John Galliano, autumn/winter 2008
PHOTOGRAPHER Patrick Demarchelier
MODEL Natalia Vodianova with (left to right)
Marina Prevot, Cristina Batista, Laurence
Morel, Béatrice Mignon, Nadège Guenin,
Monique Bailly, Florence Chehet, Gérard
Avakian, Lilly Nassar, Raffaele Ilardo, Maria-
Isabelle Bertrand and Danielle Coulon
from the Dior ateliers
FASHION EDITOR Grace Coddington
MAGAZINE *Vogue* USA, Oct. 2008
(pp. 290–91)
Patrick Demarchelier/*Vogue*; © Condé Nast

PAGE 26
COLLECTION Christian Dior haute couture
by John Galliano, autumn/winter 2007
(*Gisele Bündchen by Irving Penn* suit)
PHOTOGRAPHER Patrick Demarchelier
MODEL Caroline Trentini
FASHION EDITOR Sarajane Hoare
MAGAZINE *Vanity Fair* US, Sept. 2009 (p. 189)
Patrick Demarchelier/Vanity Fair;
© Condé Nast

PAGE 29
COLLECTION Christian Dior haute couture
by Gianfranco Ferré, spring/summer 1995
(*Silicée* dress)
PHOTOGRAPHER Mario Testino
MODEL Amber Valletta
FASHION EDITOR Carine Roitfeld
MAGAZINE *Vogue* Paris, Mar. 1995 (p. 169)
© Mario Testino

PAGES 30–31
COLLECTION Christian Dior ready-to-wear by Raf Simons, spring/summer 2013
PHOTOGRAPHER Willy Vanderperre
MODEL Daria Strokous
FASHION EDITOR Olivier Rizzo
MAGAZINE *AnOther Magazine*, spring/summer 2013 (pp. 328–29)
© Willy Vanderperre

PAGE 38
COLLECTION Christian Dior haute couture, spring/summer 1955 (*Agacerie* ensemble, A line)
PHOTOGRAPHER Henry Clarke
MODEL Anne Saint Marie
MAGAZINE *Vogue* Paris, Mar. 1955 (p. 117)
© Henry Clarke, Coll. Musée Galliera, Paris/ADAGP, Paris and DACS, London 2015

PAGE 39
COLLECTION Christian Dior haute couture, spring/summer 1953 (*Tulipe* line)
PHOTOGRAPHER Louise Dahl-Wolfe
MODEL Suzy Parker
MAGAZINE *Harper's Bazaar*, Apr. 1953 (p. 132)
Louise Dahl-Wolfe/Courtesy Staley-Wise Gallery New York. © Center for Creative Photography, The University of Arizona Foundation/DACS, 2015

PAGE 33
COLLECTION Christian Dior haute couture by Marc Bohan, spring/summer 1977
PHOTOGRAPHER Helmut Newton
MODELS Kathy Belmont, Gunilla Lindblad, Jerry Hall and unidentified models
MAGAZINE *Vogue* Paris, Mar. 1977 (p. 188)
© Estate of Helmut Newton/Maconochie Photography

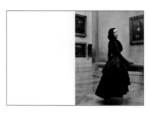

PAGE 41
COLLECTION Christian Dior haute couture by John Galliano, spring/summer 2011
PHOTOGRAPHER Annie Leibovitz
MODEL Katy Perry
FASHION EDITOR Jessica Diehl
MAGAZINE *Vanity Fair* US, June 2011 (p. 162)
© Annie Leibovitz/Contact Press Images

PAGE 34
COLLECTION Christian Dior haute couture by Marc Bohan, autumn/winter 1962
PHOTOGRAPHER Richard Avedon
MODELS Suzy Parker with Mike Nichols
MAGAZINE *Harper's Bazaar*, Sept. 1962 (unpublished image)
© The Richard Avedon Foundation

PAGES 42–43
COLLECTION Christian Dior haute couture, spring/summer 1953 (*Tulipe* line)
PHOTOGRAPHER Georges Dambier
MODEL Bettina
MAGAZINE *Elle*, 2 Mar. 1953 (unpublished variant, p. 28)
© Georges Dambier

PAGE 36
COLLECTION Christian Dior haute couture, autumn/winter 1951 (*Mexique* dress, *Longue* line)
PHOTOGRAPHER Louise Dahl-Wolfe
MODEL Mary-Jane Russell
MAGAZINE *Harper's Bazaar*, Oct. 1951 (p. 189)
Louise Dahl-Wolfe/Courtesy Staley-Wise Gallery New York. © Center for Creative Photography, The University of Arizona Foundation/DACS, 2015

PAGE 45
COLLECTION Christian Dior haute couture by John Galliano, spring/summer 1999
PHOTOGRAPHER Arthur Elgort
MODEL Audrey Marnay
FASHION EDITOR Grace Coddington
MAGAZINE *Vogue* USA, Mar. 1999 (p. 388)
Arthur Elgort/*Vogue*; © Condé Nast

PAGES 46–47
COLLECTION Christian Dior haute couture,
spring/summer 1948 (*Cocotte* dress, *Zig-Zag*
line)
PHOTOGRAPHER Clifford Coffin
MODEL unidentified (probably Anne Moffatt)
MAGAZINE *Vogue* UK, Apr. 1948 (p. 51)
© Clifford Coffin/Trunk Archive

PAGE 55
COLLECTION Christian Dior haute couture
by Gianfranco Ferré, autumn/winter 1989
(*Adagio* and *Boldini* dresses)
PHOTOGRAPHER Peter Lindbergh
MODELS Cordula Reyer and Naomi Campbell
MAGAZINE *Vogue* Paris, Sept. 1989 (cover)
© Peter Lindbergh

PAGES 48–49
COLLECTION Christian Dior haute couture,
spring/summer 1956 (hat from the *Raout*
silhouette, *Flèche* line)
PHOTOGRAPHER Henry Clarke
MODEL Dovima
MAGAZINE *Vogue* USA, 1 Apr. 1956
(unpublished variant, p. 87)
Roger-Viollet/Topfoto. © Henry Clarke, Coll.
Musée Galliera, Paris/ADAGP, Paris and DACS,
London 2015

PAGES 56–57
COLLECTION Christian Dior haute couture
by Marc Bohan, 1962
PHOTOGRAPHER Franz Christian Gundlach
MODEL unidentified
© F.C. Gundlach

PAGES 50–51
COLLECTION Christian Dior haute couture
by Marc Bohan, autumn/winter 1988
PHOTOGRAPHER Peter Lindbergh
MODEL Linda Evangelista
FASHION EDITOR Nicoletta Santoro
MAGAZINE *Vogue* Paris, Sept. 1988
(pp. 192–93)
© Peter Lindbergh

PAGE 59
COLLECTION Christian Dior haute couture
by Gianfranco Ferré, autumn/winter 1995
(*Vénus, sœur d'azur* dress)
PHOTOGRAPHER Jeanloup Sieff
MODEL Inès Rivero
MAGAZINE *Elle* US, 1995
© Estate of Jeanloup Sieff

PAGES 52–53
COLLECTION Christian Dior haute couture,
autumn/winter 1952 (*Profilée* line)
PHOTOGRAPHER Henry Clarke
MODEL Bettina
MAGAZINE *Vogue* USA, 15 Nov. 1952 (p. 99)
Condé Nast Archive/Corbis. © Henry Clarke,
Coll. Musée Galliera, Paris/ADAGP, Paris and
DACS, London 2015

PAGE 60
COLLECTION Christian Dior haute couture
by John Galliano, autumn/winter 1998
(*Mariée Zephir* dress)
PHOTOGRAPHER Patrick Demarchelier
MODEL Maggie Rizer
FASHION EDITOR Brana Wolfe
MAGAZINE *Harper's Bazaar*, Oct. 1998 (p. 243)
© Patrick Demarchelier – Hearst/Trunk
Archive

PAGES 62–63
COLLECTION Christian Dior haute couture, autumn/winter 1952 (*Esther* dress, *Profilée* line)
PHOTOGRAPHER Patrick Demarchelier
MODEL Julia Saner
FASHION EDITOR Barbara Martelo
© Patrick Demarchelier

PAGE 71
COLLECTION Christian Dior haute couture by Gianfranco Ferré, spring/summer 1994 (*Arcobaleno* dress)
PHOTOGRAPHER Mario Testino
MODEL Phoebe O'Brien
FASHION EDITOR Alexia Silvagni
MAGAZINE *Glamour* France, Mar. 1994 (p. 99)
© Mario Testino

PAGE 65
COLLECTION Christian Dior haute couture by Raf Simons, autumn/winter 2012
PHOTOGRAPHER Alasdair McLellan
MODEL Kati Nescher
FASHION EDITOR Katy England
MAGAZINE *Vogue* Paris, Sept. 2012 (p. 358)
© Alasdair McLellan

PAGES 72–73
COLLECTION Christian Dior haute couture by Yves Saint Laurent, spring/summer 1960 (*Nuit de Singapour* and *Nuit de Rio* models, *Silhouette de demain* line)
PHOTOGRAPHER William Klein
MODELS Fidelia, Victoire, Simone d'Aillencourt, Kouka and Carla Marlier
MAGAZINE *Vogue* Paris, Mar. 1960 (p. 189)
© William Klein

PAGES 66–67
COLLECTION Christian Dior haute couture by Raf Simons, autumn/winter 2013
PHOTOGRAPHER Willy Vanderperre
MODEL Elise Crombez
FASHION EDITOR Olivier Rizzo
MAGAZINE *Dior Magazine*, winter 2013 (pp. 22–23)
© Willy Vanderperre

PAGES 74–75
COLLECTION Christian Dior haute couture by Raf Simons, spring/summer 2014
PHOTOGRAPHER Mario Sorrenti
MODEL Anja Rubik with the Twins, Frankie Perez, Adrian, Rachelle, Melissa, Austin, Amber and Bonnie Malak
FASHION EDITOR Emmanuelle Alt
MAGAZINE *Vogue* Paris, May 2014 (pp. 170–71)
© Mario Sorrenti

PAGE 68
COLLECTION Christian Dior haute couture, autumn/winter 1955 (*Soirée de Paris* dress, Y line)
PHOTOGRAPHER Richard Avedon
MODEL Dovima
MAGAZINE *Harper's Bazaar*, Sept. 1955 (p. 215)
© The Richard Avedon Foundation

PAGE 76
COLLECTION Christian Dior haute couture by Gianfranco Ferré, autumn/winter 1994 (*Admata* model)
PHOTOGRAPHER Nick Knight
MODEL Christy Turlington
FASHION EDITOR Lucinda Chambers
MAGAZINE *Vogue* UK, Oct. 1994 (p. 167)
© Nick Knight/Trunk Archive

PAGE 77
COLLECTION Christian Dior haute couture by Marc Bohan, spring/summer 1966
PHOTOGRAPHER Guy Bourdin
MODEL Nicole de la Margé
MAGAZINE *Vogue* Paris, Mar. 1966 (p. 181)
© Estate of Guy Bourdin. Reproduced by permission of Art + Commerce

PAGE 78
COLLECTION Christian Dior ready-to-wear
by John Galliano, autumn/winter 2002
PHOTOGRAPHER David Sims
MODEL Yana Verba
FASHION EDITOR Anna Cockburn
MAGAZINE *Harper's Bazaar*, Sept. 2002
(p. 387)
© David Sims/Trunk Archive

PAGE 79
COLLECTION Christian Dior haute couture
by Marc Bohan, autumn/winter 1975
PHOTOGRAPHER Norman Parkinson
MODEL Jerry Hall
MAGAZINE *Vogue* UK, 1 Sept. 1975 (pp. 80–81)
© Norman Parkinson Ltd/Courtesy Norman
Parkinson Archive

PAGE 81
COLLECTION Christian Dior haute couture,
autumn/winter 1950 (*Marinette* dress,
Oblique line)
PHOTOGRAPHER Irving Penn
MODEL Régine d'Estribaud
FASHION EDITOR Bettina Ballard
MAGAZINE *Vogue* USA, 1 Sept. 1950 (p. 138)
Irving Penn/*Vogue*; © Condé Nast

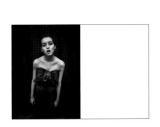

PAGE 82
COLLECTION Christian Dior haute couture
by Gianfranco Ferré, autumn/winter 1993
(*Lucie* model)
PHOTOGRAPHER Mario Sorrenti
MODEL Michele Hicks
FASHION EDITOR Alexia Silvagni
MAGAZINE *Glamour* France, Sept. 1993 (p. 125)
© Mario Sorrenti

PAGE 85
COLLECTION Christian Dior ready-to-wear
by Raf Simons, autumn/winter 2013
PHOTOGRAPHERS Inez Van Lamsweerde
& Vinoodh Matadin
MODEL Sui He
FASHION EDITOR Nicoletta Santoro
MAGAZINE *Vogue* China, Sept. 2013 (cover)
© Inez Van Lamsweerde & Vinoodh Matadin/
Trunk Archive

PAGES 86–87
COLLECTION Christian Dior haute couture
by Raf Simons, spring/summer 2014
PHOTOGRAPHER Willy Vanderperre
MODEL Stella Tennant
FASHION EDITOR Olivier Rizzo
MAGAZINE *Dior Magazine*, summer 2014
(pp. 80–81)
© Willy Vanderperre

PAGE 88
COLLECTION Christian Dior haute couture,
autumn/winter 1954 (*Gazette du bon ton*
dress, *H* line)
PHOTOGRAPHER Clifford Coffin
MODEL Marilyn Ambrose
MAGAZINE *Vogue* Paris, Sept. 1954 (p. 49)
© Clifford Coffin/*Vogue* Paris

PAGE 89
COLLECTION Christian Dior haute couture
by John Galliano, spring/summer 2004
PHOTOGRAPHER David Sims
MODEL Alexandra Tomlinson
FASHION EDITOR Marie-Amélie Sauvé
MAGAZINE *Vogue* Paris, December 2006–
January 2007 (p. 247)
© David Sims/Trunk Archive

PAGES 90–91
COLLECTION Christian Dior haute couture
by John Galliano, spring/summer 2007
(*Emi-San* dress)
PHOTOGRAPHER Greg Kadel
MODEL Anja Rubik
FASHION EDITOR Giovanna Battaglia
MAGAZINE *Vogue* China, Apr. 2007 (pp. 318–19)
© Greg Kadel/Trunk Archive

PAGE 92
COLLECTION Christian Dior haute couture,
spring/summer 1997 (*Ambrosy* dress)
PHOTOGRAPHER David Sims
MODEL Linda Evangelista
FASHION EDITOR Tonne Goodman
MAGAZINE *Harper's Bazaar*, Mar. 1997 (p. 316)
© David Sims/Trunk Archive

PAGE 93
COLLECTION Christian Dior haute couture
by Yves Saint Laurent, autumn/winter 1960
(*Moderato Cantabile* dress, *Souplesse,
légèreté, vie* line)
PHOTOGRAPHER William Klein
MODEL Dorothea MacGowan with Little Bara
MAGAZINE *Vogue* USA, 15 Sept. 1960 (p. 150)
© William Klein

PAGE 94
COLLECTION Christian Dior haute couture, autumn/winter 1951 (*Turquie* dress, *Longue* line)
PHOTOGRAPHER Cecil Beaton
MODEL Gigi
MAGAZINE *Vogue* Paris, Oct. 1951 (p. 72)
© Cecil Beaton/*Vogue* Paris

PAGE 95
COLLECTION Christian Dior haute couture by John Galliano, spring/summer 1997 (*Paloma* dress)
PHOTOGRAPHER Peter Lindbergh
MODEL Kiara Kabukuru
FASHION EDITORS Alice Gentilucci and Anna Dello Russo
MAGAZINE Supplement *Vogue* Italia, Mar. 1997 (p. 203)
© Peter Lindbergh

PAGES 96–97
COLLECTION Christian Dior haute couture by John Galliano, spring/summer 2011
PHOTOGRAPHER Nick Knight
MODEL Ming Xi
FASHION EDITOR Jonathan Kaye
MAGAZINE *V*, May–June 2011 (pp. 90–91)
© Nick Knight/Trunk Archive

PAGES 98–99
COLLECTION Christian Dior haute couture by Marc Bohan, spring/summer 1986
PHOTOGRAPHER Snowdon
MODEL Leslie Stratton with dancers José Blanche and Charles-Henry Tissot
MAGAZINE *Vogue* Paris, Mar. 1986 (pp. 318–19)
© Lord Snowdon/Trunk Archive

PAGES 100–101
COLLECTION Christian Dior haute couture, autumn/winter 1954 (*Curaçao* dress, *H* line)
PHOTOGRAPHER Henry Clarke
MODEL Victoire
MAGAZINE *Vogue* Paris, Sept. 1954 (p. 48)
Henry Clarke/*Vogue* Paris. © Henry Clarke, Coll. Musée Galliera, Paris/ADAGP, Paris and DACS, London 2015

PAGE 102
COLLECTION Christian Dior haute couture, spring/summer 1955 (*Allegro* dress, *A* line)
PHOTOGRAPHER Louise Dahl-Wolfe
MODEL Mary-Jane Russell
MAGAZINE *Harper's Bazaar*, Apr. 1955 (p. 130)
Louise Dahl-Wolfe/Courtesy Staley-Wise Gallery New York © Center for Creative Photography, The University of Arizona Foundation/DACS, 2015

PAGE 103
COLLECTION Christian Dior haute couture by Gianfranco Ferré, autumn/winter 1989 (*Walt* suit)
PHOTOGRAPHER Albert Watson
MODEL Cabrielle Reece
© Albert Watson

PAGE 104
COLLECTION Christian Dior haute couture autumn/winter 1949, autumn/winter 1949 (*Ciseaux* and *Camaïeu* dresses, *Milieu du siècle* line)
PHOTOGRAPHER Horst P. Horst
MODELS unidentified
MAGAZINE *Vogue* USA, 15 Sept. 1949 (unpublished variant, p. 136)
Horst P. Horst/*Vogue*; © Condé Nast

PAGE 105
COLLECTION Christian Dior ready-to-wear by Raf Simons, spring/summer 2013
PHOTOGRAPHER Inez Van Lamsweerde & Vinoodh Matadin
MODEL Saskia de Brauw
FASHION EDITOR Géraldine Saglio
MAGAZINE *Vogue* Paris, Mar. 2013 (p. 368)
© Inez Van Lamsweerde & Vinoodh Matadin/ Trunk Archive

PAGE 106
COLLECTION Christian Dior haute couture, autumn/winter 1948 (*Sèvres* dress, *Ailée* line)
PHOTOGRAPHER Clifford Coffin
MODEL Barbara Goalen
MAGAZINE *Vogue* USA, 1 Sept. 1948 (p. 163)
© Clifford Coffin/Trunk Archive

PAGE 107
COLLECTION Christian Dior haute couture by Gianfranco Ferré, autumn/winter 1991 (*Lux* model)
PHOTOGRAPHER Patrick Demarchelier
MODEL Linda Evangelista
FASHION EDITOR Sarajane Hoare
MAGAZINE *Vogue* UK, Oct. 1991 (p. 191)
© Patrick Demarchelier – *Vogue* UK/Trunk Archive

PAGE 109
COLLECTION Christian Dior – New York, spring/summer 1950 (*Barometer* dress)
PHOTOGRAPHER Irving Penn
MODEL Dorian Leigh
FASHION EDITOR Babs Simpson
MAGAZINE *Vogue* USA, 1 Jan. 1950 (p. 95)
Irving Penn/*Vogue*; © Condé Nast

PAGES 110–111
COLLECTION Christian Dior haute couture
by Raf Simons, spring/summer 2014
PHOTOGRAPHER Willy Vanderperre
MODEL Jessica Stam
FASHION EDITOR Marie Chaix
MAGAZINE *Vogue* China, Apr. 2014 (pp. 50–51)
© Willy Vanderperre

PAGE 118
COLLECTION Christian Dior haute couture
by Raf Simons, autumn/winter 2013
PHOTOGRAPHER David Sims
MODEL Edie Campbell
FASHION EDITOR Grace Coddington
MAGAZINE *Vogue* USA, Sept. 2013 (p. 811)
© David Sims/Trunk Archive

PAGE 112
COLLECTION Christian Dior haute couture
by Raf Simons, spring/summer 2013
PHOTOGRAPHER Paolo Roversi
MODEL Mariacarla Boscono
FASHION EDITOR Panos Yiapanis
MAGAZINE Supplement *Vogue* Italia,
Mar. 2013 (p. 71)
© Paolo Roversi/Art + Commerce

PAGES 120–121
COLLECTION Christian Dior haute couture,
autumn/winter 1949 (*Vénus* and *Junon*
dresses, *Milieu du Siècle* line)
PHOTOGRAPHER Richard Avedon
MODELS Theo Graham and unidentified
model
MAGAZINE *Harper's Bazaar*, Oct. 1949 (p. 133)
© The Richard Avedon Foundation

PAGE 115
COLLECTION Christian Dior haute couture
by Gianfranco Ferré, autumn/winter 1992
(*Ardent désir* and *Adieux* dresses)
PHOTOGRAPHER Dominique Issermann
MODELS Claudia Mason, John Foster
and Heather Stewart-Whyte
FASHION EDITOR Martine de Menthon
MAGAZINE *Vogue* Paris, Sept. 1992 (p. 160)
© Dominique Issermann/Trunk Archive

PAGES 122–123
COLLECTION Christian Dior haute couture
by John Galliano, spring/summer 2011
PHOTOGRAPHER Mario Testino
MODEL Karmen Pedaru with soldiers
of the Household Cavalry Regiment
FASHION EDITOR Lucinda Chambers
MAGAZINE *Vogue* UK, May 2011 (pp. 148–49)
© Mario Testino

PAGES 116–117
COLLECTION Special creation Christian Dior
haute couture, 1951
PHOTOGRAPHER Cecil Beaton
MODEL The Hon. Daisy Fellowes with James
Caffery
MAGAZINE *Vogue* USA, 15 Oct. 1951
(pp. 94–95)
© Condé Nast Archive/Corbis

PAGES 124–125
COLLECTION Christian Dior haute couture,
spring/summer 1948 (*Adélaide* ensemble,
Envol line)
PHOTOGRAPHER Clifford Coffin
MODEL Wenda Rogerson
MAGAZINE *Vogue* UK, Apr. 1948 (p. 56)
Clifford Coffin/*Vogue* © The Condé Nast
Publications Ltd

PAGE 127
COLLECTION Christian Dior haute couture
by John Galliano, spring/summer 1997
(*Kamata* dress)
PHOTOGRAPHER Michael Thompson
MODEL Kylie Bax
FASHION EDITOR Marcus von Ackermann
MAGAZINE *Vogue* Paris, Mar. 1997 (cover)
© Michael Thompson/Trunk Archive

PAGES 134–135
COLLECTION Special creation Christian Dior
haute couture by John Galliano, 2006
PHOTOGRAPHER Nick Knight
MODEL Gisele Bündchen
FASHION EDITOR Kate Phelan
MAGAZINE *Vogue* UK, Nov. 2006 (pp. 224–25)
© Nick Knight/Trunk Archive

PAGES 128–129
COLLECTION Christian Dior haute couture
by John Galliano, spring/summer 2007
(*Ciao-Ci-San* dress)
PHOTOGRAPHER Nick Knight
MODEL Jourdan Dunn
FASHION EDITOR Kate Phelan
MAGAZINE *Vogue* UK, Dec. 2008 (pp. 262–63)
© Nick Knight/Trunk Archive

PAGES 136–137
COLLECTION Christian Dior ready-to-wear
by Raf Simons, autumn 2015
PHOTOGRAPHER Steven Klein
MODEL Rihanna
FASHION EDITOR Mel Ottenberg
© Steven Klein

PAGE 130
COLLECTION Special creation Christian Dior
haute couture, 1949
PHOTOGRAPHER Horst P. Horst
MODEL Joan Peterkin
MAGAZINE *Vogue* USA, Dec. 1949 (p. 92)
© Condé Nast Archive/Corbis

PAGES 138–139
COLLECTION Christian Dior haute couture,
autumn/winter 1948 (*Coquette* dress,
Ailée line)
PHOTOGRAPHER Clifford Coffin
MODEL Wenda Rogerson
MAGAZINE *Vogue* USA, 15 Oct. 1948
(unpublished variant, p. 96)
© Clifford Coffin/Trunk Archive

PAGES 132–133
COLLECTIONS Christian Dior haute couture by
Raf Simons, spring/summer 2013; Christian Dior
haute couture, autumn/winter 1956 (*Salzbourg*
dress, *Aimant* line); Christian Dior haute couture,
autumn/winter 1954 (*Grand dîner* dress, *H* line);
Christian Dior haute couture by Raf Simons,
spring/summer 2013; Christian Dior–New York,
c. 1956; Christian Dior haute couture by Raf
Simons, spring/summer 2013; Christian Dior
haute couture by Raf Simons, autumn/winter
2013; Christian Dior haute couture, spring/summer
1950 (*Francis Poulenc* dress, *Verticale* line)
PHOTOGRAPHER Jean-Baptiste Mondino
MODELS Ashleigh Good, Milana Kruz, Larissa
Hofmann, Anmari Botha, Franciska Gall, Marine
Deleeuw, Devon Windsor and Sasha Luss
FASHION EDITOR Friquette Thévenet
MAGAZINE *Vanity Fair* France, Mar. 2014 (pp. 182–83)
© Jean-Baptiste Mondino

PAGES 140–141
COLLECTION Christian Dior ready-to-wear
by Raf Simons, autumn/winter 2013
PHOTOGRAPHER Peter Lindbergh
MODELS Saskia de Brauw with Daft Punk
FASHION EDITORS Aleksandra Woroniecka
and Florentine Pabst
MAGAZINE *M Le Monde*, 7 Dec. 2013 (pp. 116–17)
© Peter Lindbergh

PAGE 142
COLLECTION Christian Dior haute couture
by Marc Bohan, spring/summer 1961
(*Soirée à Lima* dress)
PHOTOGRAPHER William Klein
MODEL Simone d'Aillencourt
MAGAZINE *Vogue* Paris, Apr. 1961 (p. 148)
© William Klein

PAGE 150
COLLECTION Christian Dior haute couture
by Gianfranco Ferré, autumn/winter 1992
(*Rouge amoureuse* model)
PHOTOGRAPHER David Seidner
MODEL Helena Barquilla
FASHION EDITOR Anne-Séverine Liotard
MAGAZINE *Vogue* Paris, Sept. 1992 (p. 190)
David Seidner/*Vogue* Paris. © International
Center of Photography, David Seidner Archive

PAGE 151
COLLECTION Christian Dior haute couture,
spring/summer 1949 (*Trianon* dress,
Trompe-l'œil line)
PHOTOGRAPHER Lillian Bassman
MODEL Barbara Mullen
MAGAZINE *Harper's Bazaar,* Apr. 1949
(unpublished variant, p. 120)
Lillian Bassman/Courtesy Staley-Wise Gallery
New York

PAGE 145
COLLECTION Christian Dior haute couture
by Gianfranco Ferré, spring/summer 1996
(*Belle jeunesse* dress)
PHOTOGRAPHER Mario Testino
MODEL Kylie Bax
FASHION EDITOR Carine Roitfeld
MAGAZINE *Vogue* Paris, Mar. 1996 (p. 149)
© Mario Testino

PAGES 152–153
COLLECTION Christian Dior haute couture
by John Galliano, autumn/winter 2004
PHOTOGRAPHER Tim Walker
MODEL Lisa Cant
FASHION EDITOR Kate Phelan
MAGAZINE *Vogue* UK, Dec. 2004 (pp. 274–75)
© Tim Walker

PAGES 146–147
COLLECTION Christian Dior haute couture
by John Galliano, autumn/winter 2010
PHOTOGRAPHER Mario Sorrenti
MODEL Freja Beha Erichsen with Alexandre
Gilet and David Gallois
FASHION EDITOR Emmanuelle Alt
MAGAZINE *Vogue* Paris, Oct. 2010 (p. 534)
© Mario Sorrenti

PAGES 154–155
COLLECTION Christian Dior haute couture
by John Galliano, spring/summer 1997
(*Lina* dress)
PHOTOGRAPHER Paolo Roversi
MODEL Tasha Tilberg
FASHION EDITOR Alice Gentilucci
MAGAZINE Supplement *Vogue* Italia,
Mar. 1997 (pp. 240–41)
© Paolo Roversi/Art + Commerce

PAGE 148
COLLECTION Christian Dior haute couture
by Gianfranco Ferré, spring/summer 1995
(*Didon* model)
PHOTOGRAPHER Bruce Weber
MODEL Shalom Harlow
FASHION EDITOR Grace Coddington
MAGAZINE *Vogue* USA, Mar. 1995 (p. 384)
© Bruce Weber/Trunk Archive

PAGE 156
COLLECTION Christian Dior haute couture,
spring/summer 1950 (*Mozart* dress,
Verticale line)
PHOTOGRAPHER Norman Parkinson
MODEL Maxime de la Falaise
MAGAZINE *Vogue* USA, 1 Apr. 1950 (p. 95)
© Norman Parkinson Ltd/Courtesy Norman
Parkinson Archive

PAGE 158
COLLECTION Christian Dior haute couture, autumn/winter 1947 (*Libellule* dress, *Corolle* line)
PHOTOGRAPHER Louise Dahl-Wolfe
MODEL unidentified
MAGAZINE *Harper's Bazaar*, Dec. 1947 (p. 114)
Louise Dahl-Wolfe © Center for Creative Photography, The University of Arizona Foundation/DACS, 2015

PAGE 159
COLLECTION Christian Dior haute couture by John Galliano, autumn/winter 2007 (*Vlada Roslyakova Inspired by Sargent* dress)
PHOTOGRAPHER Tim Walker
MODEL Kate Moss and Lady Elizabeth Longman
FASHION EDITOR Katie Grand
MAGAZINE *Love*, autumn/winter 2012 (p. 416)
© Tim Walker

PAGES 160–161
COLLECTION Christian Dior haute couture spring/summer 1950, spring/summer 1950 (*Schumann* dress, *Verticale* line)
PHOTOGRAPHER Louise Dahl-Wolfe
MODEL Simone Arnal
MAGAZINE *Harper's Bazaar*, Mar. 1950 (unpublished variant, p. 35)
Louise Dahl-Wolfe/Courtesy Staley-Wise Gallery New York. © Center for Creative Photography, The University of Arizona Foundation/DACS, 2015

PAGE 162
COLLECTION Christian Dior haute couture, autumn/winter 1952 (*Palmyre* dress, *Profilée* line)
PHOTOGRAPHER Henry Clarke
MODEL unidentified
MAGAZINE *Vogue* USA, 15 Nov. 1952 (p. 102)
© Condé Nast Archive/Corbis

PAGE 163
COLLECTION Christian Dior haute couture, autumn/winter 1952 (*Palmyre* dress, *Profilée* line)
PHOTOGRAPHER Juergen Teller
MODEL Stephanie Seymour
FASHION EDITOR Joe Zee
MAGAZINE *W*, Dec. 1999 (p. 265)
© Juergen Teller. Andy Warhol artworks © 2015 The Andy Warhol Foundation for the Visual Arts, Inc./Artists Rights Society (ARS), New York and DACS, London

PAGE 164
COLLECTION Christian Dior haute couture by John Galliano, autumn/winter 2009
PHOTOGRAPHER Paolo Roversi
MODEL Darya Kurovska
FASHION EDITOR Alex White
MAGAZINE *W*, Oct. 2009 (p. 175)
© Paolo Roversi/Art + Commerce

PAGES 166–167
COLLECTIONS Dior Joaillerie by Victoire de Castellane, 2006 (*Ingénue* necklace), and Christian Dior ready-to-wear by John Galliano, autumn/winter 2006
PHOTOGRAPHERS Inez Van Lamsweerde & Vinoodh Matadin
MODEL Raquel Zimmermann
FASHION EDITOR Emmanuelle Alt
MAGAZINE *Vogue* Paris, Aug. 2006 (p. 158)
© Inez Van Lamsweerde & Vinoodh Matadin/ Trunk Archive

PAGE 168
COLLECTION Christian Dior haute couture by Marc Bohan, autumn/winter 1979
PHOTOGRAPHER Horst P. Horst
MODEL unidentified
MAGAZINE *Vogue* Paris, Sept. 1979 (p. 413)
© Horst P. Horst/*Vogue* Paris

PAGE 169
COLLECTION Christian Dior haute couture by Raf Simons, autumn/winter 2014
PHOTOGRAPHER Paolo Roversi
MODEL Kasia Jujeczka
FASHION EDITOR Robbie Spencer
MAGAZINE Supplement *Vogue* Italia, Sept. 2014 (p. 48)
© Paolo Roversi/Art + Commerce

PAGES 170–171
COLLECTION Christian Dior haute couture, autumn/winter 1954 (*Zémire* dress, *H* line)
PHOTOGRAPHER Clifford Coffin
MODEL Nancy Berg
MAGAZINE *Vogue* Paris, Sept. 1954 (p. 48)
© Clifford Coffin/Trunk Archive

PAGE 173
COLLECTION Christian Dior haute couture by Raf Simons, autumn/winter 2014
PHOTOGRAPHER Gregory Harris
MODEL Kinga Rajzak
FASHION EDITOR Caroline Newell
MAGAZINE *Dior Magazine*, winter 2014 (p. 22)
© Gregory Harris/Trunk Archive

PAGES 174–175
COLLECTION Christian Dior haute couture
by Marc Bohan, autumn/winter 1963
(*Inès* dress), slipper by Roger Vivier
PHOTOGRAPHER Richard Avedon
MAGAZINE *Harper's Bazaar*, Sept. 1963 (p. 226)
© The Richard Avedon Foundation

PAGE 183
COLLECTION Christian Dior haute couture
by Raf Simons, autumn/winter 2014
PHOTOGRAPHER Tom Ordoyno
MODEL Lena Hardt
FASHION EDITOR Tallulah Harlech
MAGAZINE *Pop*, autumn/winter 2014 (p. 442)
© Tom Ordoyno

PAGE 176
COLLECTION Christian Dior haute couture
by John Galliano, spring/summer 2008
PHOTOGRAPHER Paolo Roversi
MODEL Freja Beha Erichsen
FASHION EDITOR Jacob K.
MAGAZINE Supplement *Vogue* Italia,
Mar. 2008 (p. 191)
© Paolo Roversi/Art + Commerce

PAGE 177
COLLECTION Christian Dior ready-to-wear
by Gianfranco Ferré, autumn/winter 1990
PHOTOGRAPHER Peter Lindbergh
MODEL Kim Williams
FASHION EDITOR Babeth Djian
MAGAZINE *Vogue* Paris, Nov. 1990 (p. 222)
© Peter Lindbergh

PAGES 184–185
COLLECTION Christian Dior haute couture
by Raf Simons, autumn/winter 2014
PHOTOGRAPHER Paolo Roversi
MODEL Natalia Vodianova
FASHION EDITOR Robbie Spencer
MAGAZINE *Vogue* Russia, Dec. 2014
(pp. 228–29)
© Paolo Roversi/Art + Commerce

PAGE 179
COLLECTION Christian Dior haute couture
by Gianfranco Ferré, spring/summer 1992
(*Jardin aux Roses* dress)
PHOTOGRAPHER Dominique Issermann
MODEL Heather Stewart-Whyte
FASHION EDITOR Martine de Menthon
MAGAZINE *Vogue* Paris, Mar. 1992 (p. 179)
© Dominique Issermann/Trunk Archive

PAGE 186
Princess Margaret
COLLECTION Special creation Christian Dior
haute couture, 1951
PHOTOGRAPHER Cecil Beaton
© Victoria & Albert Museum, London/
Cecil Beaton Archive

PAGES 180–181
COLLECTION Christian Dior haute couture
by John Galliano, autumn/winter 1997
(*Maharani Krishna Kumari du Népal* dress)
PHOTOGRAPHER Ellen von Unwerth
MODEL Michele Hicks
FASHION EDITOR Alice Gentilucci
MAGAZINE Supplement *Vogue* Italia,
Sept. 1997 (pp. 264–65)
© Ellen von Unwerth/Trunk Archive

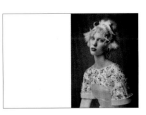

PAGE 189
COLLECTION Christian Dior haute couture
by Raf Simons, spring/summer 2013
PHOTOGRAPHER Patrick Demarchelier
MODEL Juliana Schurig
FASHION EDITOR Edward Enninful
MAGAZINE *W* US, May 2013 (p. 165)
© Patrick Demarchelier – Condé Nast US/
Trunk Archive

PAGE 190
COLLECTION Special creation Christian Dior haute couture, 1951
PHOTOGRAPHER Cecil Beaton
MODEL Virginia Ryan
MAGAZINE *Vogue* USA, 1 Mar. 1951 (p. 177)
Cecil Beaton/*Vogue*; © Condé Nast

PAGE 191
COLLECTION Christian Dior ready-to-wear by Raf Simons, spring/summer 2014
PHOTOGRAPHER Tyrone Lebon
MODELS Georgia May Jagger and Charlotte Free
FASHION EDITOR Francesca Burns
MAGAZINE *Vogue* UK, Mar. 2014 (p. 373)
© Tyrone Lebon

PAGES 192–193
COLLECTION Christian Dior haute couture by Gianfranco Ferré, autumn/winter 1994 (*Ailée* model)
PHOTOGRAPHER Juergen Teller
MODEL Kristen McMenamy
FASHION EDITOR Jenny Capitain
MAGAZINE *Vogue* Paris, Sept. 1994 (pp. 200–1)
© Juergen Teller

PAGE 194
COLLECTION Christian Dior haute couture by Gianfranco Ferré, spring/summer 1996 (*Ballet de fleurs* dress)
PHOTOGRAPHER Paolo Roversi
MODEL Guinevere Van Seenus
FASHION EDITOR Alice Gentilucci
MAGAZINE Supplement *Vogue* Italia, Mar. 1996 (p. 204)
© Paolo Roversi/Art + Commerce

PAGES 196–197
COLLECTION Christian Dior haute couture by John Galliano, spring/summer 2001
PHOTOGRAPHER Mario Testino
MODEL Marina Dias
FASHION EDITOR Lucinda Chambers
MAGAZINE *Vogue* UK, Apr. 2001 (pp. 248–49)
© Mario Testino

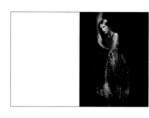

PAGE 199
COLLECTION Christian Dior haute couture by Raf Simons, spring/summer 2013
PHOTOGRAPHER Paolo Roversi
MODEL Malgosia Bela
FASHION EDITOR Panos Yiapanis
MAGAZINE Supplement *Vogue* Italia, Mar. 2013 (p. 83)
© Paolo Roversi/Art + Commerce

PAGES 200–201
COLLECTION Christian Dior haute couture by Marc Bohan, autumn/winter 1976
PHOTOGRAPHER Barry Lategan
MODEL Sue Purdy
MAGAZINE *Vogue* UK, 1 Sept. 1976 (pp. 94–95)
Barry Lategan/*Vogue* © The Condé Nast Publications Ltd

PAGE 202
Princess Margaret
COLLECTION Special design Christian Dior haute couture, 1951
PHOTOGRAPHER Cecil Beaton
© Victoria & Albert Museum, London/ Cecil Beaton Archive

PAGES 204–205
COLLECTION Christian Dior haute couture by John Galliano, spring/summer 2010
PHOTOGRAPHER Paolo Roversi
MODEL Dorothea Barth-Jorgensen
FASHION EDITOR Lucinda Chambers
MAGAZINE *Vogue* UK, May 2010 (pp. 128–29)
© Paolo Roversi/Art + Commerce

PAGES 206–207
COLLECTION Christian Dior haute couture
by Marc Bohan, autumn/winter 1985
PHOTOGRAPHER Snowdon
MODEL Isabelle Pasco
FASHION EDITOR Grace Coddington
MAGAZINE *Vogue* UK, Sept. 1985 (p. 310)
© Lord Snowdon/Trunk Archive

PAGES 214–215
COLLECTION Christian Dior haute couture
by Marc Bohan, autumn/winter 1977
PHOTOGRAPHER Lothar Schmid
MODEL Carrie Nygren
MAGAZINE *Vogue* UK, 1 Sept. 1977 (pp. 108–9)
Lothar Schmid/*Vogue* © The Condé Nast
Publications Ltd

PAGE 208
COLLECTION Christian Dior ready-to-wear
by John Galliano, autumn/winter 2007
PHOTOGRAPHER Paolo Roversi
MODEL Daria Werbowy
FASHION EDITOR Lucinda Chambers
MAGAZINE *Vogue* UK, June 2007 (p. 144)
© Paolo Roversi/Art + Commerce

PAGE 217
COLLECTION Christian Dior haute couture
by Raf Simons, spring/summer 2013
PHOTOGRAPHER Tim Walker
MODEL Cara Delevingne
FASHION EDITOR Edward Enninful
MAGAZINE *W*, Apr. 2013 (p. 107)
© Tim Walker

PAGES 210–211
COLLECTION Christian Dior haute couture
by Raf Simons, spring/summer 2015
PHOTOGRAPHER Annie Leibovitz
MODELS Vanessa Axente, Mirte Maas,
Fei Fei Sun and Maartje Verhoef
FASHION EDITOR Grace Coddington
MAGAZINE *Vogue* USA, Apr. 2015 (p. 256)
© Annie Leibovitz/Trunk Archive

PAGE 218
COLLECTION Christian Dior haute couture
by Raf Simons, spring/summer 2014
PHOTOGRAPHER Sarah Moon
MODEL Merilin Perli
FASHION EDITOR Nicole Picart
MAGAZINE *Madame Figaro*, 14 Feb. 2014 (p. 67)
© Sarah Moon

PAGE 219
COLLECTION Christian Dior haute couture
by Raf Simons, spring/summer 2014
PHOTOGRAPHER Tom Ordoyno
MODEL Indigo Lewin
FASHION EDITOR Tallulah Harlech
MAGAZINE *Pop*, autumn/winter 2014 (p. 435)
© Tom Ordoyno

PAGES 212–213
COLLECTION Christian Dior haute couture
by Marc Bohan, spring/summer 1971
PHOTOGRAPHER Guy Bourdin
MODELS unidentified
MAGAZINE *Vogue* Paris, Mar. 1971 (p. 157)
© Estate of Guy Bourdin. Reproduced by
permission of Art + Commerce

PAGES 220–221
COLLECTION Christian Dior haute couture
by Yves Saint Laurent, spring/summer 1959
(hat from the *Raout* silhouette, *Longue* line)
PHOTOGRAPHER Guy Bourdin
MODEL Rose-Marie Cardin
MAGAZINE *Vogue* Paris, Apr. 1959 (pp. 116–17)
© Estate of Guy Bourdin. Reproduced by
permission of Art + Commerce

PAGE 223
COLLECTION Christian Dior haute couture
by Marc Bohan, autumn/winter 1976
PHOTOGRAPHER Guy Bourdin
MODEL Kathy Quirk
MAGAZINE *Vogue* Paris, Sept. 1976 (p. 202)
© Estate of Guy Bourdin. Reproduced by
permission of Art + Commerce

PAGE 231
COLLECTION Christian Dior ready-to-wear
by Raf Simons, autumn/winter 2014
PHOTOGRAPHER Bruce Weber
MODEL Eliza Cummings with Claire
Christeron and Michael Bailey Gates
FASHION EDITOR Aleksandra Woroniecka
MAGAZINE *M Le Monde*, 6 Dec. 2014 (p. 113)
© Bruce Weber/Trunk Archive

PAGE 224
COLLECTION Christian Dior haute couture
by Yves Saint Laurent, spring/summer
1960 (*Nuit de Grenade* dress, *Souplesse,
légèreté, vie* line)
PHOTOGRAPHER Patrick Demarchelier
MODEL Jac Jagaciak
FASHION EDITOR Patti Wilson
© Patrick Demarchelier

PAGE 225
COLLECTION Christian Dior ready-to-wear
by John Galliano, autumn/winter 2005
PHOTOGRAPHER Juergen Teller
MODEL Gisele Bündchen
FASHION EDITOR Jane How
MAGAZINE *W*, June 2005 (p. 145)
© Juergen Teller

PAGES 232–233
COLLECTION Christian Dior haute couture
by Raf Simons, autumn/winter 2012
PHOTOGRAPHER Paolo Roversi
MODELS Antonina Vasylchenko, Jac Jagaciak,
Daria Strokous, Kinga Rajzak, Alexandra
Martynova, Zuzanna Bijoch, Nastya Kusakina,
and Esther Heesch
FASHION EDITOR Jessica Diehl
MAGAZINE *Vanity Fair* US, Sept. 2012
(pp. 338–39)
© Paolo Roversi/Art + Commerce

PAGE 226
COLLECTION Dior Joaillerie by Victoire de
Castellane, 2007 (*Dracula Spinella Devorus*
and *Paradisea Cœur Secretus* rings,
Belladone Island collection)
PHOTOGRAPHER Mario Sorrenti
MODEL Lara Stone
FASHION EDITOR Carine Roitfeld
MAGAZINE *Vogue* Paris, Apr. 2007 (p. 250)
© Mario Sorrenti

PAGE 234
COLLECTION Christian Dior haute couture
by John Galliano, autumn/winter 1997
(*Princesse Partabgarh* ensemble)
PHOTOGRAPHER Annie Leibovitz
MODEL Nicole Kidman
FASHION EDITOR Nicoletta Santoro
MAGAZINE *Vanity Fair* US, Oct. 1997 (p. 317)
© Annie Leibovitz/Contact Press Images

PAGES 228–229
COLLECTION Christian Dior – New York,
spring/summer 1964
PHOTOGRAPHER Bert Stern
MODEL Wilhelmina
MAGAZINE *Vogue* USA, 1 Feb. 1964 (cover)
© Condé Nast Archive/Corbis

PAGE 237
COLLECTION Christian Dior haute couture
by John Galliano, spring/summer 1998
(hat from the *Cunard Line* silhouette)
PHOTOGRAPHER Mikael Jansson
MODEL Karen Elson
FASHION EDITOR Sarajane Hoare
MAGAZINE *Frank*, July 1998 (p. 82)
© Mikael Jansson/Trunk Archive

PAGE 238
COLLECTION Christian Dior haute couture by John Galliano, autumn/winter 1997 (*Princesse Bundi* and *Princesse Partabgarh* ensembles)
PHOTOGRAPHER Patrick Demarchelier
MODELS Danielle Zinaich and Kylie Bax
FASHION EDITOR Sarajane Hoare
MAGAZINE *Harper's Bazaar* US, Oct. 1997 (p. 190)
© Patrick Demarchelier – Hearst/Trunk Archive

PAGE 239
COLLECTION Christian Dior haute couture by John Galliano, autumn/winter 1999
PHOTOGRAPHER Nathaniel Goldberg
MODEL Stella Tennant
FASHION EDITOR Samuel François
MAGAZINE *Numéro*, Dec. 1999–Jan. 2000 (p. 167)
© Nathaniel Goldberg/Trunk Archive

PAGES 240–241
COLLECTION Christian Dior haute couture by John Galliano, autumn/winter 1997
PHOTOGRAPHER Irving Penn
MODEL Kirsty Hume
FASHION EDITOR Phyllis Posnick
MAGAZINE *Vogue* USA, Oct. 1997 (pp. 396–97)
Irving Penn/Vogue; © Condé Nast

PAGE 243
COLLECTION Christian Dior ready-to-wear by John Galliano, autumn/winter 2008
PHOTOGRAPHER Camilla Akrans
MODEL Mariacarla Boscono
FASHION EDITOR Sissy Vian
MAGAZINE *Vogue* Japan, Mar. 2009 (p. 228)
© Camilla Åkrans. Courtesy Management + Artists

PAGES 244–245
PHOTOGRAPHER Cecil Beaton
MODEL Mitzah Bricard
Courtesy of the Cecil Beaton Studio Archive at Sotheby's

PAGES 246–247
COLLECTION Christian Dior haute couture, spring/summer 1957 (*Libre* line)
PHOTOGRAPHER Henry Clarke
MODEL Joanna McCormick
MAGAZINE *Vogue* Paris, Mar. 1957 (unpublished variant, p. 119)
Henry Clarke/Vogue Paris. © Henry Clarke, Coll. Musée Galliera, Paris/ADAGP, Paris and DACS, London 2015

PAGE 248
COLLECTION Christian Dior haute couture by John Galliano, autumn/winter 2008
PHOTOGRAPHER Terry Richardson
MODEL Lara Stone
FASHION EDITOR George Cortina
MAGAZINE *Vogue* Japan, Oct. 2008 (p. 314)
© Terry Richardson

PAGE 250
COLLECTION Christian Dior ready-to-wear by John Galliano, autumn/winter 2007
PHOTOGRAPHER Camilla Akrans
MODEL Sasha Pivovarova
FASHION EDITOR Franck Benhamou
MAGAZINE *Numéro*, Sept. 2007 (cover)
© Camilla Åkrans. Courtesy Management + Artists

PAGE 251
COLLECTION Christian Dior haute couture, spring/summer 1947 (*Maxim's* dress, *Corolle* line)
PHOTOGRAPHER Horst P. Horst
MODEL Rita Hayworth
Horst P. Horst/© Condé Nast. Courtesy Victoria and Albert Museum, London

PAGE 252
COLLECTION Christian Dior haute couture by John Galliano, autumn/winter 2005 (*Vivien* dress)
PHOTOGRAPHER Paolo Roversi
MODEL Eva Herzigova
MAGAZINE *Vogue* Japan, Dec. 2005 (p. 124)
© Paolo Roversi/Art + Commerce

PAGE 253
COLLECTION Christian Dior haute couture by John Galliano, autumn/winter 2005 (*Ginger* dress)
PHOTOGRAPHER Paolo Roversi
MODEL Shalom Harlow
MAGAZINE *Vogue* Japan, Dec. 2005 (p. 125)
© Paolo Roversi/Art + Commerce

PAGE 254
COLLECTION Christian Dior haute couture, autumn/winter 1947 (*Chandernagor* dress, *Corolle* line)
PHOTOGRAPHER Horst P. Horst
MODEL Marlene Dietrich
MAGAZINE *Vogue* USA, 1 Jan. 1948 (unpublished variant, p. 144)
Marlene Dietrich/*Vogue*; © Condé Nast

PAGE 256
COLLECTION Christian Dior haute couture by Gianfranco Ferré, spring/summer 1994 (*Cambremer* model)
PHOTOGRAPHER Dominique Issermann
MODEL Nadja Auermann
FASHION EDITOR Martine de Menthon
MAGAZINE *Vogue* Paris, 1 Mar. 1994 (p. 175)
© Dominique Issermann/Trunk Archive

PAGE 257
COLLECTION Christian Dior haute couture by Gianfranco Ferré, autumn/winter 1992
PHOTOGRAPHER Max Vadukul
MODEL Tatjana Patitz
FASHION EDITOR Lucinda Chambers
MAGAZINE *Vogue* UK, Oct. 1992 (p. 178)
© Max Vadukul/AUGUST

PAGES 258–259
COLLECTION Christian Dior ready-to-wear by John Galliano, spring/summer 2010
PHOTOGRAPHER Luciana Val & Franco Musso
MODEL Elsa Sylvan
FASHION EDITOR Capucine Safyurtlu
MAGAZINE *Numéro*, Apr. 2008 (pp. 158–59)
© Luciana Val & Franco Musso

PAGES 260–261
COLLECTION Christian Dior – New York, autumn/winter 1962
PHOTOGRAPHER Bert Stern
MODEL Marilyn Monroe
FASHION EDITOR Babs Simpson
MAGAZINE *Vogue* US, 1 Sept. 1962 (unpublished variant, p. 191)
Marilyn Monroe, from the Last Sitting, 1962. Bert Stern/Courtesy Staley-Wise Gallery New York

PAGE 263
COLLECTION Special creation Christian Dior haute couture, 2012
PHOTOGRAPHER Patrick Demarchelier
MODEL Charlize Theron
© Patrick Demarchelier

PAGES 264–265
COLLECTION Christian Dior ready-to-wear by Raf Simons, spring/summer 2014
PHOTOGRAPHER Paolo Roversi
MODEL Natalie Portman
FASHION EDITOR Kate Young
MAGAZINE *Dior Magazine*, spring 2014 (unpublished variant, pp. 32–33)
© Paolo Roversi/Art + Commerce

PAGE 266
COLLECTION Christian Dior haute couture by Raf Simons, autumn/winter 2012
PHOTOGRAPHER Tim Walker
MODEL Marion Cotillard
FASHION EDITOR Jacob K.
MAGAZINE *W* US, Dec. 2012 (cover)
© Tim Walker

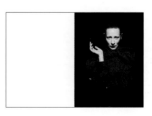

PAGE 269
COLLECTION Christian Dior ready-to-wear by Raf Simons, autumn/winter 2013 (*Arizona* 1948 coat)
PHOTOGRAPHER Willy Vanderperre
MODEL Cate Blanchett
FASHION EDITOR Olivier Rizzo
MAGAZINE *AnOther Magazine*, autumn/winter 2013 (p. 365)
© Willy Vanderperre

PAGES 270–271
COLLECTION Christian Dior haute couture, autumn/winter 1948 (*Arizona* coat, *Ailée* line)
PHOTOGRAPHER Jean-Baptiste Mondino
MODEL Marion Cotillard
FASHION EDITOR Friquette Thévenet
MAGAZINE *Dior Magazine*, autumn 2012 (pp. 30–31)
© Jean-Baptiste Mondino

PAGE 279
COLLECTION Christian Dior haute couture by John Galliano, autumn/winter 1997 (earring from the *Princesse Lucknow* silhouette)
PHOTOGRAPHER Irving Penn
MODEL Carolyn Murphy
FASHION EDITOR Phyllis Posnick
MAGAZINE *Vogue* USA, Dec. 1997 (unpublished image)
Copyright © The Irving Penn Foundation

PAGE 272
COLLECTION Christian Dior ready-to-wear by Raf Simons, autumn/winter 2014
PHOTOGRAPHER Mario Testino
MODEL Suvi Koponen
FASHION EDITOR Sarajane Hoare
MAGAZINE *Vogue* Japan, Nov. 2014 (p. 213)
© Mario Testino

PAGE 280
COLLECTION Christian Dior – London, autumn/winter 1956
PHOTOGRAPHER Norman Parkinson
MODEL Barbara Mullen
MAGAZINE *Vogue* UK, Nov. 1956 (p. 84)
© Norman Parkinson Ltd/Courtesy Norman Parkinson Archive

PAGE 281
COLLECTION Christian Dior haute couture by Gianfranco Ferré, autumn/winter 1996 (*Shalimar* dress)
PHOTOGRAPHER Gilles Bensimon
MODEL Honor Fraser
FASHION EDITOR Fanny Pagniez
MAGAZINE *Elle* US, Oct. 1996 (p. 281)
© Gilles Bensimon

PAGES 274–275
COLLECTION Christian Dior ready-to-wear by John Galliano, autumn/winter 2007
PHOTOGRAPHERS Mert Alas & Marcus Piggott
MODEL Lara Stone
FASHION EDITOR Alex White
MAGAZINE *W*, Sept. 2007 (p. 537)
© Mert Alas & Marcus Piggott

PAGES 282–283
COLLECTION Christian Dior – New York, spring/summer 1952 (*Frisson* dress)
PHOTOGRAPHER Frances McLaughlin
MODEL Suzy Parker
MAGAZINE *Vogue* USA, 1 Mar. 1952 (p. 144)
© Condé Nast Archive/Corbis

PAGE 277
COLLECTION Christian Dior fur by Frédéric Castet, autumn/winter 1976
PHOTOGRAPHER Helmut Newton
MODEL Sylvia Kristel
MAGAZINE *Vogue* Paris, Nov. 1976 (p. 126)
© Estate of Helmut Newton/Maconochie Photography

PAGES 284–285
COLLECTION Christian Dior haute couture by John Galliano, spring/summer 2007 (*Dolore-San* dress)
PHOTOGRAPHER Nick Knight
MODEL Kate Moss
FASHION EDITOR Kate Phelan
MAGAZINE *Vogue* UK, Dec. 2008 (cover)
© Nick Knight/Trunk Archive

PAGE 286
COLLECTION Christian Dior haute couture
by Raf Simons, autumn/winter 2013
PHOTOGRAPHER Willy Vanderperre
MODEL Elise Crombez
FASHION EDITOR Olivier Rizzo
MAGAZINE *Style.com*, spring 2014 (p. 117)
© Willy Vanderperre

PAGE 287
COLLECTION Christian Dior haute couture,
spring/summer 1950 (*Francis Poulenc*
dress, *Verticale* line)
PHOTOGRAPHER Norman Parkinson
MODEL Jean Patchett
MAGAZINE *Vogue* UK, May 1950
(unpublished variant, p. 94)
© Norman Parkinson Ltd/Courtesy
Norman Parkinson Archive

PAGE 289
COLLECTION Christian Dior haute couture
by Raf Simons, autumn/winter 2014
PHOTOGRAPHER Benjamin Alexander
Huseby
MODEL Amanda Murphy
FASHION EDITOR Jodie Barnes
MAGAZINE *V* US, winter 2014 (p. 102)
© Benjamin Alexander Huseby

PAGES 290–291
COLLECTION Christian Dior haute couture
by Raf Simons, autumn/winter 2012
PHOTOGRAPHER Peter Lindbergh
MODEL Milla Jovovich
FASHION EDITOR Jacob K.
MAGAZINE Supplement *Vogue* Italia,
Sept. 2012 (pp. 62–63)
© Peter Lindbergh. Jenny Holzer, H.C.
Experimental, 2012, © Jenny Holzer. ARS,
NY and DACS, London 2015

ACKNOWLEDGMENTS

This book would not have been possible without the invaluable support of Patrick Mauriès, who first read the text for Thames & Hudson.

The author wishes to thank Olivier Bialobos, Mathilde Favier-Meyer, Hélène Poirier, Philippe Le Moult, Soizic Pfaff, Perrine Scherrer, Hélène Starkman, Daphné Catroux, Laurence Despouys, Leïla El Blida, Stéphanie Pélian, Kelly Fakret, Beatrice Piovella, Gilberto Sacchi, Lucy Xu and Noemie Dong at Christian Dior, and also Antje Campe-Thieling, Stephanie Betz and Elisa Apicella.

Additional thanks to Victor Martin, Christine Boubée, Brigitte Tortet, Jo Walton, Stéphane Moll and Gail de Courcy-Ireland.

Special thanks to Mario Testino for his trust.

On the cover: Photo © Willy Vanderperre.
Model: Suvi Koponen courtesy of DNA Model Management

First published in the United Kingdom in 2015 by Thames & Hudson Ltd,
181A High Holborn, London WC1V 7QX

This reduced format edition 2022

First published in the United States of America in 2015 by Harper Design,
an Imprint of HarperCollins Publishers, New York

This reduced format edition first published in the United States
of America in 2022 by Thames & Hudson Inc., 500 Fifth Avenue,
New York, New York 10110

Reprinted 2024

Dior: New Looks © 2015 and 2022 Thames & Hudson Ltd, London
Text © Jérôme Gautier
Translated from the French by Gail de Courcy-Ireland

British Library Cataloguing-in-Publication Data
A catalogue record for this book is available from the British Library

Library of Congress Control Number 2021942689

ISBN 978-0-500-02504-8

Printed in China by, Artron Art (Group) Co., Ltd.

FSC
www.fsc.org
MIX
Paper from
responsible sources
FSC® C019910

Be the first to know about our new releases,
exclusive content and author events by visiting
thamesandhudson.com
thamesandhudsonusa.com
thamesandhudson.com.au